Practice in

Spanish Grammar

for students starting post-16 courses

Mark Cholij

With thanks to my wife Martha Ramirez-Ramos Cholij and my sister Lidia Cholij for all
their help and support, and to my children Michelle and Dominic.

Text © Mark Cholij, 1996

Original line illustrations © Stanley Thornes (Publishers) Ltd 1996

First published in 1996 by Stanley Thornes (Publishers) Ltd
Reprinted in 2003 by:
Nelson Thornes Ltd
Delta Place,
27 Bath Road,
CHELTENHAM GL53 7TH
United Kingdom

03 04 05 06 07 / 10 9 8

A catalogue record for this book is available from the British Library.

ISBN 0 7487 2376 5

Illustrations by John Taylor
Typeset by Tech-Set, Gateshead, Type and Wear
Printed in Croatia by Zrinski

Contents

Introduction

Practice in Spanish Grammar gives a comprehensive introduction to the full range of grammar required for speaking and writing Spanish at a higher level. It also provides an intensive revision programme for those students who are preparing to take a higher level examination in Spanish in the near future.

As well as offering an opportunity to consolidate and practise systematically the main areas of Spanish grammar, *Practice in Spanish Grammar* is designed to be used as a reference book at any stage of a higher level course in Spanish. For this reason there is a full index at the back. You will also notice that, after an area of grammar has been practised, an Extra Reference section is supplied for further study.

Unless you have already completed an advanced course in Spanish, it is best to work systematically through *Practice in Spanish Grammar* in the order provided by the units. Since this book has been designed primarily for self-study, you will find an Answer Section at the back.

At the end of each unit you will find a progress test. Do not proceed to the next unit until it has been completed (satisfactorily!).

At the beginning of each unit you will find a dialogue which sets the tone for the unit and contains, in context, the grammar to be discussed and practised. As well as including new grammar, each dialogue deliberately incorporates grammar that has been previously practised or remarked upon in another unit. Accordingly, these dialogues should be read very carefully.

Where possible, humour has been 'injected' into the dialogues and practice exercises to make the grammar less dry. Remember, however, that the real fun of a language is to be able to dominate its grammar so that you are able to write and speak both confidently and fluently. Hard work now will pay great dividends later on. When you learn a language properly, you learn it for life.

Guide to grammatical terms

Most grammatical terms used in this book are explained in context as you come across them. Before beginning this course, however, you should check below that you are familiar with some of the more basic terms.

1 Sentence structure

i) a = subject; b = verb; c = direct object.

   a   b   c   a   b   c
Miguel opened the door. = *Miguel abrió la puerta.*

ii) a = direct object; b = indirect object.

          b   a   a   b
We gave Pedro a present. = *Le dimos un regalo a Pedro.*

iii) a = transitive verb; b = direct object; c = intransitive verb.

A transitive verb is one that takes a direct object. An intransitive verb is one that does not take a direct object.

          a   b   a   b
My brother missed the flight. = *Mi hermano perdió el vuelo.*

         c   c
The plane landed. = *El avión aterrizó.*

iv) a = subject; b = active verb; c = passive verb.

The words active/passive refer to the form of a verb. In the active, the action is done by the subject. In the passive, the action is done to the subject.

   a   b   a   b
Carmen wrote the letter. = *Carmen escribió la carta.*

   a   c   a   c
The letter was written by Carmen. = *La carta fue escrita por Carmen.*

Although the passive form of the verb is very common in English, it is usually avoided in Spanish.

v) a = Infinitive.

         a   a
She wants to come with us. = *Ella quiere venir con nosotros.*

vi) a = 1st person singular (verb); b = 2nd person singular (verb);
c = 3rd person plural (verb).

<pre>
     a   b   c   a   b
  I know, you know; but do they know? = Yo sé, tú sabes,

         c
  pero ¿saben ellos?
</pre>

2 Parts of speech

i) a = pronoun; b = noun.

A pronoun replaces a noun.

<pre>
   a   b   a   b
  She didn't see the man. = Ella no vio al hombre.

         b   a   b   a
  The policeman arrested him. = El policía le arrestó.
</pre>

ii) a = subject pronoun; b = direct object pronoun.

<pre>
    a   b   a   b
  She cleaned it. = Ella lo limpió.

   a   b   a b
  I saw her. = Yo la vi.
</pre>

iii) a = subject pronoun; b = indirect object pronoun.

<pre>
     a   b   a   b
  They spoke to me. = Ellos me hablaron.
</pre>

iv) a = definite article; b = indefinite article; c = noun.

<pre>
    a   c   a   c
  The house is new. = La casa es nueva.

         b   c   b   c
  It is a new house. = Es una casa nueva.
</pre>

v) a = adjective; b = noun.

An adjective is a word that tells us more about a noun.

<pre>
               a   b   b   a
  It's an interesting book. = Es un libro interesante.
</pre>

vi) a = adverb; b = verb; c = adjective.

An adverb gives more information about a verb or an adjective. It can also be used to comment on a whole sentence.

<pre>
      a   b   a   a   b   a
Generally, I   drive slowly. = Generalmente, conduzco   despacio.
</pre>

<pre>
      b   a   c   b   a   c
He   is seriously ill. = Está gravemente enfermo.
</pre>

vii) a = preposition.

<pre>
       a   a
It's on   the   floor. = Está en el suelo.
</pre>

There are four things you need to bear in mind when dealing with prepositions:

1 In front of **el, de** and **a** become **del** and **al**.

   detrás del restaurante = behind the restaurant
   al principio = at first

2 Spanish and English prepositions do not necessarily correspond.

   at home = *en casa*
   on the right = *a la derecha*

3 In English we can replace a standard verb with a phrasal verb (= a combination of two words which has a single meaning.)

   eg explode = blow up ; extinguish = put out; test = try out/on.
   In Spanish, however, there are no phrasal verbs.
   explode = *estallar(se)*; extinguish = *apagar*; test = *probar*.

4 In Spanish, **a** before a *person* object noun is obligatory.

   No conozco a sus padres. = I don't know his parents.

UNIT 1 Reacting to people and situations

Pilar and Marta, both seventeen, are on holiday in the northern town of
Torrelavega. They have decided to spend Saturday night at 'La Juerga'
discotheque. They are sitting at a table.

Pilar: ¡Qué calor hace aquí! Este sitio es un horno. Y,   1.1; 1.3;
¡qué música más pesada! No me gusta esta   1.1; 1.4 / 1.3
discoteca. Vámonos a otro sitio.

Marta: Pero, ¿adónde? No hay otra discoteca por aquí y   1.2
los bares están llenos. ¿Por qué no nos quedamos   1.2; 1.6
un rato más a ver qué pasa? ¿Quieres tomar algo?   1.6

Pilar: De momento no. Tengo ganas de bailar pero la
música no me anima.   1.6

Marta: Yo sé lo que te hace falta. Mira: ¿no te parece   1.5 / 1.3
guapo aquel chico que está sentado junto a la
entrada?

Pilar: ¿Cuál? ¿El de la camiseta azul oscuro?   1.2

Marta: Sí. ¿No te llama la atención?   1.6

Pilar: Pues sí, no está mal. Pero, ¡qué cara tan seria   1.1
tiene! ¿No le notas que está como enojado?   1.6

Marta: Sí, es cierto. Parece fastidiado. Algo pasa entre él   1.5; 1.6
y el otro muchacho: el rubio que lleva la chaqueta   1.6

        de cuero. Fíjate cómo se <u>miran</u> el uno al otro. ¡Se   1.6
        han puesto de pie! ¡Están a punto de pelearse!

Pilar: Seguro que tiene algo que ver con <u>esa chica</u> que   1.3
        está con   ellos. Mira la cara de ella. <u>¡Qué pálida</u> 1.1
        <u>está!</u>

Marta: ¡Dios mío! El rubio ha sacado una navaja. ¡Ay!
        <u>¡qué miedo! ¿Qué hace ese loco?</u> Pilar, ¿qué   1.1; 1,3; 1.6
        <u>hacemos?</u>

1.1 Using ¡qué! in exclamations.

¡Qué calor hace! ¡Qué música más pesada!
¡Qué cara tan seria tiene! ¡Qué pálida está! ¡Qué miedo!

Although forming exclamations with **¡qué!** appears quite straightforward, there are some important differences between English and Spanish usage that should be carefully noted.

- **What a (+ noun)! = ¡Qué (+ noun)!**

  In English, we say: What a man!   What a surprise!

  In Spanish, **¡Qué!** is never followed by **un** or **una**: *¡Qué hombre! ¡Qué sorpresa!*

- **How (+ adjective)! = ¡Qué (+ adjective)!**

  In English, we say: How nice (she is)!   How easy (it is)!

  In Spanish, **¡qué!** (not **¡cómo!**) is used: *¡Qué simpática (es)! ¡Qué fácil (es)!*

- **Be very careful when you use ¡qué! with an adjective + noun.**

  In English, we say: What a stupid man!   What an ugly dog!

  In Spanish, however, **más** or **tan** is placed in front of an adjective that follows a noun. *¡Qué hombre más tonto! ¡Qué perro tan feo!*

  However, if you use a phrase where the adjective goes before the noun then you do not need to use **más** or **tan**.

  A good idea.   = *Una buena idea.*

  What a good idea! = *¡Qué buena idea!*

Practice (1): Forming appropriate exclamations with ¡qué!

Form ten appropriate exclamations by combining the words below.

¡Qué bien	*tienes!*
¡Qué bebé	*cantas!*
¡Qué suerte	*más perezoso!*
¡Qué hombre	*hace aquí dentro!*
¡Qué fuerte	*parecen!*
¡Qué felices	*más bonitos!*
¡Qué chica	*tan lindo!*
¡Qué ojos	*más guapa!*
¡Qué frío	*más fácil!*
¡Qué ejercicio	*eres!*

Practice (2): Recognising and using fixed phrases with ¡qué!

Look at the following situations and select an appropriate exclamation for each one.

1) You are in a restaurant. A person sitting at the next table is slurping and munching his way through his meal, wiping his mouth with the back of his hand and burping every two minutes. What might you say (to yourself or your companion)?

    a *¡Qué precioso!*

    b *¡Qué asco!*

    c *¡Qué divertido!*

2) You have been waiting for almost an hour in the pouring rain for your boyfriend/girlfriend to turn up. What might you be thinking?

    a *¡Qué risa!*

    b *¡Qué día tan espléndido!*

    c *¡Qué rabia!*

3) Unfortunately, you are unable to accept an invitation to a friend's wedding because of a prior engagement. What might you or your friend say?

    a *¡Qué lástima!*

    b *¡Qué bien!*

    c *¡Qué tontería!*

4) You thought you had lost a folder containing revision notes for an important examination. Then you find the folder underneath your bed. What might you say?

    a *¡Qué pena!*

    b *¡Qué horror!*

    c *¡Qué alivio!*

5) You are at a very formal party where everybody is dressed up. Your companion, however, is wearing dirty jeans and has obviously not had a bath for a week. Everybody is staring at him/her. What might you be thinking?

    a *¡Qué susto!*

    b *¡Qué vergüenza!*

    c *¡Qué emocionante!*

6) A student in your class is always making sarcastic remarks about others. His jokes are cruel and he takes pleasure in hurting others. What sort of comment might you make?

    a *¡Qué simpático es!*

    b *¡Qué sensible es!*

    c *¡Qué antipático es!*

Extra reference

Alternative words to **¡qué!**:

✦ In spoken Spanish, you will often hear **¡vaya!** instead of **¡qué!** when the speaker wishes to express surprise/wonder or a negative sentiment.

¡Vaya suerte!	= How lucky can you get!
¡Vaya tío!	= What a bloke/man!
¡Vaya coche!	= What a car!
¡Vaya servicio!	= What (bad) service!

✦ You should also note the use of **menudo** when somebody is being ironical.

¡Menudo plan!	= Some plan! (*I don't think much of it.*)
¡Menuda idea!	= What an idea! (*I'm not impressed.*)

✦ **¡Cómo!** is used in exclamations that depend on a verb.

¡Cómo te quiero!	= How I love you!
¡Cómo le odio!	= How I hate him!

1.2 Revising basic question words

¿Adónde? ¿Por qué? ¿Cuál? ¿Qué?

Further on in this book, we shall be dealing with some of the problems involved in selecting the most appropriate question word. Before doing so, however, it is well worth revising basic question words and their use in context.

When using question words do not forget the following:

● A question word must carry an accent. ¿Quién? (Who?) ¿Cuándo? (When?)

● A question is indicated by two question marks, the first being placed at the point where the question actually starts. In other words, the first question mark does not have to be at the beginning of a sentence.

Pero, ¿qué haces?
But, what are you doing?

Y, ¿dónde está?
And, where is it?

● Use ¿adónde? (not ¿dónde?) if **where?** actually means **where to?**.

¿Adónde quieres ir?
Where do you want to go (to)?

Practice (3): Recognising when to use a particular question word

Selecting from the following words, complete each question below.
**Cuánto Cuántos Cuál Cómo Cuándo Dónde Adónde
Por dónde Qué A qué En qué De qué Para qué Por qué
Quién De quién**

1 —¿........ está Consuelo?
   —Se ha ido a la tienda.
2 —¿........ vas?
   —A la farmacia.
3 —¿........ se va a la estación?
   —Se va por esa calle.

4 —¿........ *color es?*
—*Azul.*

5 —¿........ *parte de Madrid vives?*
—*En el sur.*

6 —¿........ *vale?*
—*Doscientas pesetas.*

7 —¿........ *quiere?*
—*Seis, por favor.*

8 —¿........ *prefiere, la verde o la amarilla?*
—*La verde.*

9 —¿........ *desea?*
—*Un kilo de patatas, por favor.*

10 —¿........ *es este abrigo?*
—*Es de mi hermana.*

11 —¿........ *es?*
—*Es mi hermano mayor.*

12 —¿........ *sirve este aparato?*
—*Para limpiar la piscina.*

13 —¿........ *hora empieza la película?*
—*A las cinco y media.*

14 —¿........ *te sientes?*
—*Un poquito mejor, gracias.*

15 —¿........ *ocurrió eso?*
—*Ayer.*

16 —¿........ *no te gusta la escuela?*
—*Porque me aburro.*

Is it ¿qué? or ¿cómo?

Extra reference

Does a question word still carry an accent if it is in the middle of a sentence? The answer is yes, if it is a question word.

✦ A question word will carry an accent irrespective of whether the question is a direct one or an indirect one. If an indirect question is part of a statement, the question word will still carry an accent.

a) *¿De dónde sale el agua?*
   Where is the water coming out from?

   ¿Sabes de dónde sale el agua?
   Do you know where the water is coming out from?

   Yo no sé de dónde sale el agua.
   I don't know where the water is coming out from.

b) *¿Quién es?*
   Who is it?

   ¿Sabes quién es?
   Do you know who it is?

   No sabemos quién es.
   We don't know who it is.

1.3 Distinguishing between **este, ese** and **aquel.**

este sitio   esta discoteca   aquel chico   esa chica   ese loco

● **This or that? (¿Este o ese?)**

Usually when distinguishing between **this** and **that**, one uses **este** (this) and **ese** (that). The full form of these words is as follows:

	This	These	That	Those
(masculine)	*este*	*estos*	*ese*	*esos*
(feminine)	*esta*	*estas*	*esa*	*esas*

Este vestido vale quince mil pesetas; ese vestido vale veinte mil.
This dress costs 15,000 pesetas; that dress costs 20,000.

Esta camisa está sucia, pero esa camisa está limpia.
This shirt is dirty, but that shirt is clean.

● There is, however, another word in Spanish for **that: aquel**

Aquel also means **that,** in the sense of 'that...over there'. The full form of the word is as follows:

	That	**Those**
(masculine)	*aquel*	*aquellos*
(feminine)	*aquella*	*aquellas*

¿Qué vestido prefiere? ¿Este vestido verde? ¿Ese vestido blanco? O, ¿aquel vestido negro?
Which dress do you prefer? This green dress? That white dress? Or that black dress (over there)?

● What is the difference between **ese** and **aquel?**

In general terms, **aquel** has the idea of remoteness and distance.

¿Te acuerdas de aquel chico que ...?
Do you remember that boy who ...?

En aquel año ...
(In) that year ...

● When do we need to place an accent on **este, ese, aquel?**

When you want to say **this one, that one, these ones** or **those ones,** you don't actually need to translate the word **one.** The usual practice, however, is to place an accent on **este, ese** and **aquel** when they have this meaning.

éste/éstos   ése/ésos   aquél/aquéllos
ésta/éstas   ésa/ésas   aquélla/aquéllas

It is not actually obligatory to use accents with these words (unless there is a definite possibility of confusion), but most educated writers do.

—*¿Te gusta este vestido?*	– Do you like this dress?
—*Prefiero ése.*	– I prefer that one.
—*¿Cuál? ¿Éste azul?*	– Which one? This blue one?
—*No, ése amarillo.*	– No, that yellow one.

● **What is the difference between este and esto?**

It is important not to confuse **este/ese/aquel** with **esto/eso/ aquello**. When referring to an idea, a whole statement or anything not specifically mentioned by name, you should use **esto/eso/ aquello** to translate **this/that**.

¿Qué es esto?	= What's this?
¿Qué quiere decir esto?	= What does this mean?

Las hembras de los mamíferos alimentan a sus crías con leche que sale de su propio cuerpo. Ninguna otra clase de animales puede hacer <u>esto</u>; sólo los mamíferos.
Female mammals feed their young with milk that comes from their own body. No other class of animal can do <u>this</u>; only mammals.

Eso es.
That's right/That's it.

Eso es cierto.
That's right/true.

Eso sí que es verdad.
That's certainly true.
(NB: The use of **sí** to emphasise a word is an extremely important device in spoken Spanish, eg —*Ahora <u>sí</u> (que) entiendo.* = <u>Now</u> I understand.)

Aquello no tiene nada que ver con esto.
That (business in the past) has nothing to do with this (present business).

Practice (4): Knowing when to use **este, ese, aquel**

Complete the following dialogue by translating the words in brackets into Spanish.

—*Buenos días. ¿Qué desea?*
—(How much are these apples?)
—*Son a doscientas el kilo.*
—(And those ones?)
—*¿Cuáles? ¿Las verdes?*
—(Yes, those green ones.)
—*A trescientas el kilo.*
—(And those red ones over there, how much are they?)
—*Lo mismo. A trescientas el kilo.*

—¿Cuáles recomienda usted?
—¡Yo qué sé! ¡Las manzanas son manzanas, señora!
—(That's not true.) Hay manzanas buenas y manzanas malas. Hay manzanas dulces y manzanas duras.
—No tengo tiempo para discutir. ¿Quiere comprar algo o no?
—Le voy a decir una cosa. Es usted muy mal educado. En mis tiempos, los hombres eran verdaderos caballeros. Yo me acuerdo…
—(This is ridiculous!) Mire usted. ¿No ve que hay una cola de más de diez personas?
—(That is not my problem!)
—¡Usted me está sacando de quicio! ¿Quiere comprar algo o no?
—No sé. ¿Qué recomienda usted?

Extra reference

When reading Spanish, it is very important that you understand that a simple word like **este** has more than one function or meaning.

✦ For emphasis or clarification, **éste/éstos/ésta/éstas** (*note the accents!*) are often used as linking words where in English we would use **he, she, it** and **they**.

—Miguel siempre tiene sueño. ¡Éste nació cansado!
Michael's always tired. He was born tired!

Un marinero nos prestó una barca, pero ésta, al llegar a la Costa de Oro, se estrelló contra las rocas y se destrozó.
A sailor lent us a boat, but on reaching the Gold Coast it was dashed to pieces against the rocks.

✦ Why does **éste** also mean the **latter** and **aquél** mean the **former?**

Since **éste** refers to what is nearest to you and **aquél** has the idea of distance, the two words are used to translate the **latter** and the **former.**

Mis mejores amigos son Pedro y Fernando; éste es alto y rubio, aquél es bajo y moreno.
My best friends are Pedro and Fernando. The latter is tall with fair hair, and the former is short and dark-haired/skinned.

✦ If you wish to say <u>the</u> one(s), use **el/la/los/las.**

¿El de la camiseta azul oscuro?
The one with the dark blue T-shirt?

El rubio que lleva la chaqueta de cuero.
The fair-haired one wearing the leather jacket.

1.4 Using **gustar**.

No me gusta esta discoteca

● **Gustar** is an indirect verb (and, therefore, does not follow the same sentence pattern as **like** in English).

Quite a few verbs in Spanish are used in an indirect way. In grammatical terms, these verbs indicate something that is of specific interest **to** you.

Gustar can only be used in an indirect way, It is important that you learn to handle this particular verb confidently because then you can apply the same sentence pattern to other verbs.

● Look at the following examples to remind yourself of the basic patterns used with gustar.

Me gusta	= I like it. (*It pleases me.*)
Me gustan.	= I like them. (*They please me.*)
Me gusta mucho.	= I like it a lot. (*It pleases me a lot.*)
No me gusta.	= I don't like it.
Me gusta este disco.	= I like this record.
Me gustan estos discos.	= I like these records.
Me gusta viajar	= I like travelling. (Note the different verb forms)

● **What do we mean by an indirect verb?**

Quite simply, when a verb is used indirectly, it must have an indirect object pronoun before it. Look carefully at the following table:

Indirect Object Pronouns

me (to me)
te (to you)
le (to him, to her, to you <**usted**>)
nos (to us)
os (to you)
les (to them, to you <**ustedes**>)

● **If me means to me, why do the Spanish also use a mí?**

For emphasis or for clarification, an extra phrase is often placed in front of the indirect object pronoun or immediately after the verb. These phrases are: **a mí, a ti, a él, a ella, a usted, a nosotros/as, a vosotros/as, a ellos, a ellas, a ustedes.**

Look carefully at the following examples:

A ti te gusta esta música, pero a mí no (me gusta).
You like this music, but I don't .

A ella le gusta el perfume francés.
She likes French perfume.

A nosotras no nos gusta el fútbol.
We don't like football.

¿Les gusta a ustedes?
Do you like it?

● An indirect construction must always have an indirect pronoun. If you wish to name a person, you should place the indirect **A +** **name** either in front of the indirect object pronoun or immediately after the verb.

A Pedro le gusta jugar al tenis.
Pedro likes playing tennis.

A María no le gusta esa clase de música.
María doesn't like that type of music.

Practice (5): Recognising the correct sentence pattern with **gustar**

Place the following words in the correct order.

1 *clásica la música mí a gusta me*

2 *¿perros los gustan te ti a?*

3 *té el Fernando a gusta no le*

4 *bailar les gusta no ellos a*

5 *¿gusta este os vestido?*

Practice (6): Using **gustar** in context

Are the following sentences correct? Tick any sentence that is correct. Underline and correct any mistake(s) you find. In some cases, a word may be missing.

1 *¿A te ti gustas este disco?*

2 *Me gusta jugando al ajedrez en mis ratos libres.*

3 *Mi hermana le gusta tomando el sol, pero a mí no.*

4 *No me gusta verte vestida de esta manera. ¿No te da vergüenza?*

5 *A Paco no gusta estudiar.*

6 *¿Le gusta a usted el flamenco?*

7 *A mi abuelo no le gusta salir; prefiere quedarse en casa. En cambio, mi abuela se aburre en casa; ella sí la gusta salir.*

8 *Muchas personas no les gustan las arañas.*

9 *¿Cuál te gustan más, éste o ése?*

10 *¿Os gusta este vino?*

Extra reference

✦ If you wish to emphasise that you do not like something, you can either say no **me gusta mucho** (I don't like it much) or **no me gusta nada** (I don't like it at all).

✦ Which verb, **gustar** or **caer**?

Although **gustar** can be used to refer to a person (especially when referring to physical qualities), it is more natural to use **caer** when referring to somebody's personality. When **caer** means **to like**, it is used in an indirect way.

Me gusta Pedro.
I like Pedro. (*I find him physically attractive.*)

Pedro me cae bien.
I like Pedro. (*He's a nice person.*)

1.5 Using **parecer**.

No te parece guapo aquel chico...? Parece fastidiado

● **Parecer** is used so often, both in spoken and written Spanish, that it is worth taking the time to master this verb thoroughly.

i) The basic meaning of **parecer** is **to seem** (*appear/look*).

Parece difícil, pero no lo es.
It seems difficult, but it isn't.

Pareces cansado.
You look tired.

Parece que no vienen.
It seems that (*looks as if*) they are not coming.

ii) When used to make comparisons, **parecer** means **to look like** (*resemble*).

A veces es difícil distinguir lo que es y lo que no es un pez. Un caballito de mar no parece un pez; pero lo es. Y un delfín parece un pez, pero no lo es.
Sometimes it is difficult to tell what is and what isn't a fish. A sea horse doesn't look like a fish, but it is one. And a dolphin looks like a fish, but it isn't one.

iii) When used as a reflexive verb, **parecerse** means **to be like** (*look alike/take after*).

Miguel se parece mucho a su padre.
Miguel is very much like his father.

Miguel y su padre se parecen mucho.
Miguel and his father are very much alike.

Ese perro se parece a su amo.
That dog looks just like his master.

iv) When used in an indirect construction (like **gustar**), **parecer** means **to think** (*to seem to you*) — and it is this construction that you should pay particular attention to.

¿Qué te parece este reloj?
What do you think of this watch?

¿Qué tal te parece aquella chica?
What do you think of that girl?

¿No te parece guapo?
Don't you think he's good-looking?

Me parece que te has equivocado.
I think you've made a mistake.

Me parece que sí/no.
I think so/not.

Me parece caro este hotel.
I think this hotel is expensive. (NB: Note the word order.)

¿Qué te parece si vamos a otro sitio?
¿Por qué no vamos a otro sitio?

Practice (7): Knowing when to use **parecer**

Using **parecer** in each case, finish each sentence in such a way that it means exactly the same as the sentence above it.

1 *Creo que va a llover.*
   Me ....

2 *En mi opinión no es una buena idea.*
   No ....

3 *Pilar y su madre no se parecen mucho.*
   Pilar no ....

4 *¿Te gusta este disco?*
   ¿Qué tal ....?

5 *Creo que sí.*
   Me ....

6 *Con tanto maquillaje en la cara, das la impresión de ser un payaso.*
   Con tanto maquillaje en la cara, ...

7 *Aquel chico no es tan guapo como todos creen.*
   A mí no ....

8 *Para mí este libro es muy pesado.*
   Me ....

9 *¿Por qué no vamos al cine esta tarde?*
   ¿Qué ....?

10 *¡No es mucho dinero!*
   ¡Me ....!

Extra reference

Note carefully the following expressions:

Parece mentira.	= It seems incredible. / It's hard to believe.
Me parece bien.	= That's fine.
Es parecido a	= It is similar to
A mi parecer	= In my opinion
Al parecer	= Apparently

1.6 Recognising the various uses of the Present Tense (Indicative)

nos quedamos quieres anima llama notas pasa lleva miran hace hacemos

---

● Just as in English, the Present Tense in Spanish is used to (a) state facts relating to the present; (b) express general truths; and (c) describe habitual actions that occur in the present.

Las serpientes sólo comen cosas vivas.
Snakes only eat live things.

Los perros son listos y aprenden con facilidad.
Dogs are clever and learn easily.

Los inútiles siempre le echan la culpa a la herramienta.
Bad workmen always blame their tools.

Poquito a poco se llega lejos.
Slow but sure wins the race.

Siempre tomo un café después del almuerzo.
I always have a coffee after lunch.

● It is important to realize that, within specific contexts and especially in spoken Spanish, the Present Tense has a variety of functions.

i) It can denote the future:

Mañana viajo a Francia.	= Tomorrow I'm travelling to France.
Lo hago más tarde.	= I'll do it later.
¿Qué hacemos?	= What shall we do?

ii) It can be used to comment on or describe what is actually happening at the moment:

¿Qué hace ese loco?	= What's that lunatic doing?
Algo pasa.	= Something is happening. /Something is wrong.
Lleva una chaqueta de cuero.	= He's wearing a leather jacket.

iii) It can be used to express offers or suggestions:

¿Te traigo algo?	=	Shall I bring/get you something?
¿Te ayudo?	=	Shall/can I help you?
¿Vamos al cine?	=	Shall we go to the cinema?
¿Tomamos algo?	=	Shall we have something to drink?

iv) It can be used to make a request:

¿Me bajas la maleta, por favor?	=	Could you bring down my suitcase, please?
¿Me das un café, por favor?	=	Could I have a coffee?
Me pone un tinto, por favor.	=	A glass of red wine, please.
¿Me permite ver su pasaporte?	=	May I see your passport?
¿Quiere sentarse?	=	Would you like to sit down?
¿Quiere callarse?	=	Would you shut up!

v) It is used to emphasise a momentary fact:

No oigo nada.	=	I can't hear anything (*at this moment*).
No veo nada.	=	I can't see anything (*at this moment*).

vi) It is used in certain time constructions (with **llevar, acabar, hace** and **desde hace**). (See 3.1).

The more spoken Spanish you hear, the more you will realize that the Present Tense in Spanish is a very flexible tense. Accordingly, you should take particular care when translating from Spanish into English.

Practice (8): Recognising the flexibility of the Spanish Present Tense

Read the following dialogue, and then translate into appropriate English the words that have been underlined.

—*Dígame.*

—*¿Está Rosa, por favor?*

—*¿De parte de quién?*

—*Soy Lola.*

—*Un momentito, que la llamo* (1). *¡Rosa! ¡Al teléfono! Te llama Lola.*

—*¡Voy, madre!* (2)

—*Ya viene.* (3)
—*Gracias.*

....

—*Hola.*
—*Hola Rosa, soy Lola. ¿Qué tal?*
—*Bien.*
—*¿Te apetece salir* (4) *esta tarde?*
—*Pues sí. ¿Adónde vamos?* (5)
—*Al cine, si quieres.* (6)
—*Me parece bien. ¿Qué ponen?* (7)
—*"El último beso". Empieza* (8) *a las cinco y media.*
—*Está bien. Entonces, ¿a qué hora nos vemos?* (9)
—*Sobre las cinco, si te parece bien.*
—*De acuerdo. Y, ¿dónde nos encontramos?* (10)
—*En el bar 'Jorge'.*
—*Vale. Hasta luego entonces.*
—*Hasta luego.*

Practice (9)

Study the following sentences carefully, and then translate the words
that have been underlined into natural English.

1 —*¿Has visto mis gafas? No las encuentro por ninguna parte.*
    —*Aquí están, abuelita.*

2 —*Son las seis y media. Tengo que arreglarme. Mi novio viene a
    las siete a recogerme.*

3 —*¿Me ayudas con esta maleta? Es que pesa mucho.*

4 —*¿Vas a la cocina?*
    —*Sí. ¿Quieres algo?*
    —*Sí. ¿Me traes un vaso de agua, por favor? Es que no me siento bien.*

5 —*Aquí viene el camarero. ¿Qué vas a tomar?*
    —*No sé. Tú, ¿qué tomas?*
    —*Me apetece una cerveza bien fría.*

6   —¿*Qué haces,* Ramón?
    —*Nada, mamá.*
    — *¿Me haces un favor?*
    —*Por supuesto, mamá.*

7   —¿*Qué es tu padre*, Ramón?
    —*Es cartero.*

8   —*La cuenta, por favor.*
    —*La traigo ahora mismo, señor.*

Progress test 1

Translate the following items into Spanish.

  1   What a surprise!
  2   How well they dance!
  3   What a stupid man!
  4   Where are you going, Enrique?
  5   Who is that girl (*over there*)?
  6   I like these shoes.
  7   I don't like this dress, but I like that one.
  8   My brother likes that record.
  9   He doesn't like dancing.
 10   What's this?
 11   That's certainly true.
 12   What does this mean?
 13   What do you think of José?
 14   I think he's nice.
 15   I think this hotel is very expensive.

UNIT 2   Making observations

Paco, Carmen and Alicia are spending a day on the beach.

Paco: Hace un calor insoportable. Me voy a bañar.   2.1; 2.3/2.1
¿Vienes?

Alicia: Todavía no. Estoy muy a gusto bajo esta   2.1
sombrilla. Mira, allí está Carmen. ¡Carmen!,
¡que estamos aquí!   2.1

Carmen: Hola! ¿Qué tal? ¡Cómo pega el sol!, ¿eh?   2.1

Alicia: ¡Y tanto! ¿Quieres un poco de crema? Tienes la   2.1; 2.2
piel muy blanca y te vas a poner como un   2.3
cangrejo si no te proteges la piel.

Carmen: Por eso llevo este sombrero.   2.1

Alicia: Te va bien. Pero, ¿seguro que no quieres un   2.1
poco de crema?

Carmen: Gracias, de momento no.

Paco: Tengo ganas de meterme en el agua. ¿Me   2.2/2.3
acompañas, Carmen?   2.1

Carmen: Un poquito más tarde, Paco. Quiero charlar un   2.1
rato con Alicia.

Paco: Bueno, hasta luego entonces.

(Veinte minutos más tarde.)

Carmen *(riéndose)*: Me parece que Paco <u>confunde</u> el   2.1
         nadar con la lucha libre.

Alicia: ¿Por qué <u>dices</u> eso?   2.1

Carmen: Pues, míralo.

Alicia: No le <u>veo</u>. ¿Dónde está?   2.1

Carmen: Cerca de aquellas rocas. Mira cómo <u>se pelea</u> con 2.3
         el agua.

Alicia: Pero Paco no <u>nada</u> así. Él <u>sabe</u> nadar muy bien. 2.1
            ¡Ay, Dios mío! Algo le pasa. <u>¡Se ahoga!</u> ¡Se   2.3
            ahoga!

Paco: ¿Quién se ahoga?

Alicia: ¡¡Paco!!

Carmen *(para sí misma)*: <u>Necesito</u> gafas.   2.1

2.1 Forming the Present Tense (indicative)

> **hace voy estoy estamos pega quieres tienes vas llevo va tengo acompañas quiero confunde dices veo está nada sabe necesito**

- All verbs in Spanish end in -AR, -ER or -IR. Although the majority of verbs are regular in formation, there are a large number of common verbs that are irregular. There are also certain spelling rules that you need to be familiar with.

- Regular -AR verbs.
  The majority of Spanish verbs end in -AR, and most of them are regular.

	Tomar (to take)	**Usar** (to use)
yo	tomo	uso
tú	tomas	usas
él, ella, usted	toma	usa
nosotros, -as	tomamos	usamos
vosotros, -as	tomáis	usáis
ellos, -as, ustedes	toman	usan

Do not forget that it is not necessary to use subject pronouns (**yo, tú, él, ella,** etc.) in Spanish. They tend to be used either for emphasis or to avoid possible confusion.

– In English we use a helping verb (do) to make a verb negative or to make a question. In Spanish, **no** tells us that the verb is negative and question marks indicate that we are asking a question.

Do you smoke?	=	*¿Fuma usted?*
No, I don't smoke.	=	*No, no fumo.*
No, I don't.	=	*No.* (or: *No, no fumo.*)

– In English we use question tags (does he?, don't they?, will they?, did she?...etc.) when we seek confirmation of a statement. In Spanish, **¿verdad?** is used (for all tenses) as a question tag.

You smoke, don't you?	=	*Usted fuma, ¿verdad?*
You don't smoke, do you?	=	*Usted no fuma, ¿verdad?*

● **Irregular -AR verbs.**

Learn the following two verbs by heart:

dar (to give): *doy, das, da, damos, dais, dan.*

estar (to be): *estoy, estás, está, estamos, estáis, están.*

● **Regular -ER verbs.**

-ER verbs are formed in the following way:

	Meter (to put/put in)	**Vender** (to sell)
yo	*meto*	*vendo*
tú	*metes*	*vendes*
él, ella, usted	*mete*	*vende*
nosotros, -as	*metemos*	*vendemos*
vosotros, -as	*metéis*	*vendéis*
ellos, -as, ustedes	*meten*	*venden*

● **Irregular -ER verbs.**

a) Learn the following verbs by heart:

poder (to be able): *puedo, puedes, puede, podemos, podéis, pueden.*
querer (to want): *quiero, quieres, quiere, queremos, queréis, quieren.*
ser (to be): *soy, eres, es, somos, sois, son.*
tener (to have): *tengo, tienes, tiene, tenemos, tenéis, tienen.*
oler (to smell): *huelo, hueles, huele, olemos, oléis, huelen.*

b) Note that the following -ER verbs are irregular in the first person singular only.

caber (to fit): *quepo, cabes, cabe, cabemos, cabéis, caben.*
caer (to fall): *caigo, caes, cae, caemos, caéis, caen.*
hacer (to do/make): *hago, haces, hace, hacemos, hacéis, hacen.*
poner (to put): *pongo, pones, pone, ponemos, ponéis, ponen.*
saber (to know): *sé, sabes, sabe, sabemos, sabéis, saben.*
traer (to bring): *traigo, traes, trae, traemos, traéis, traen.*
valer (to be worth): *valgo, vales, vale, valemos, valéis, valen.*
ver (to see): *veo, ves, ve, vemos, veis, ven.*

c) Pay particular attention to **haber:**

haber (to have): *he, has, ha, hemos, habéis, han.*

– The Present Tense of **haber** is used to form the Present Perfect tense.

He hablado. = I have spoken. (See 4.5)

– The Present tense of **haber** is also used with **de + infinitive** to mean 'to have to/must'.

Los guardianes del zoo han de conocer muy bien a los animales para saber cuidarles.
Zoo-keepers have to know a great deal about animals in order to be able to look after them.

Los animales salvajes cazan su comida, pero los animales del zoo han de ser alimentados por sus cuidadores.
Wild animals hunt their food, but zoo animals have to be fed by their keepers.

– **Haber** also has a neutral form: **hay** (there is/there are).

– **Hay + que + infinitive** can be used to express obligation/necessity.

Hay que decirle. = It is necessary to tell him. / He must be told.

● Regular -IR verbs.

-IR verbs are formed in the following way:

	Abrir (to open)	**Sufrir** (to suffer)
yo	abro	sufro
tú	abres	sufres
él, ella, usted	abre	sufre
nosotros, -as	abrimos	sufrimos
vosotros, -as	abrís	sufrís
ellos, -as, ustedes	abren	sufren

● Irregular -IR verbs.

Learn the following by heart:

decir (to say/tell): *digo, dices, dice, decimos, decís, dicen.*

ir (to go): *voy, vas, va, vamos, vais, van.*

oír (to hear): *oigo, oyes, oye, oímos, oís, oyen.*

salir (to go out/leave): *salgo, sales, sale, salimos, salís, salen.*

venir (to come): *vengo, vienes, viene, venimos, venís, vienen.*

● **Spelling changes.**

When forming the Present Tense, certain spelling changes have to be made so that the verb retains its original pronunciation. Since Spanish is phonetic, these changes are very logical and should be noted very carefully.

a) If a verb ends in **-cer/-cir**, the first person singular will end in **-zco.**

conocer (to know): *conozco, conoces, conoce, conocemos, conocéis, conocen.*

conducir (to drive): *conduzco, conduces, conduce, conducimos, conducís, conducen.*

Further examples include: *agradecer* (to thank/be grateful for), *aparecer* (to turn up), *crecer* (to grow), *merecer* (to deserve), *obedecer* (to obey), *ofrecer* (to offer), *parecer* (to seem), *pertenecer* (to belong), *reconocer* (to recognise), *traducir* (to translate), *reducir* (to reduce).

b) If a verb ends in **-ger/-gir**, the first person singular will end in **-jo.**

coger (to take): *cojo, coges, coge, cogemos, cogéis, cogen.*

dirigir (to direct): *dirijo, diriges, dirige, dirigimos, dirigís, dirigen.*

c) If a verb ends in **-uir**, the **i** becomes **y** except for the first and second persons plural.

construir (to construct): *construyo, construyes, construye, construimos, construís, construyen.*

Further examples include: *destruir* (to destroy), *incluir* (to include), *huir* (to flee).

d) A few verbs ending in **-iar** or **-uar** may require a written accent to retain the correct sound of the verb.

enviar (to send): *envío, envías, envía, enviamos, enviáis, envían.*

continuar (to continue): *continúo, continúas, continúa, continuamos, continuáis, continúan.*

Further examples include: *confiar* (to entrust/trust), *enfriar* (to cool), *espiar* (to spy), *fiarse* (to trust), *guiar* (to guide), *fluctuar* (to fluctuate).

Practice (1): Using the present tense to give factual information

In the following extracts, four people who are associated with the sea in some way or other are talking about their jobs. For each extract, change each verb in brackets into the correct form of the Present Tense.

To check your general comprehension, you will find underneath each extract three alternatives indicating what that person's job/occupation is. Select the correct alternative.

1) *Yo (trabajar) bajo el mar. (Llevar) un pesado casco de metal que me (cubrir) toda la cabeza. El casco (ir) herméticamente unido a un traje impermeable, de modo que no (poder) entrar el agua. Un tubo flexible fijado en la parte posterior del casco (llevar) aire, para que pueda respirar.*

    a *Es minero.*

    b *Es buzo.*

    c *Es cartero.*

2) *Nosotros no (poder) realizar nuestro trabajo sin redes. Antes de hacernos a la mar, siempre (reparar) las redes para que no haya agujeros. Nuestro trabajo (ser) bastante peligroso y muy duro. Nosotros (correr) muchos riesgos, pero (ganar) muy poco dinero.*

    a *Es leñador.*

    b *Es agricultor.*

    c *Es pescador.*

3) *Mi trabajo (consistir) en rescatar a las personas en peligro. Cuando (haber) un barco en peligro, nosotros (salir) velozmente en su ayuda.*

   a *Es guardacostas.*

   b *Es guardaespaldas.*

   c *Es guardia urbano.*

4) *Yo (dar) órdenes a la tripulación y (dirigir) el rumbo del barco. (Ser) el responsable de todo cuanto (ocurrir) a bordo.*

   a *Es marinero de cubierta.*

   b *Es el capitán de un barco.*

   c *Es pastor.*

Practice (2): Using the present tense in normal speech

Complete the following dialogue by changing each verb in brackets into the correct form of the Present Tense.

—*Tú me (deber) cien mil pesetas, José. (Necesitar) el dinero hoy.*

—*Mañana, Luis. Te (prometer) que tendrás el dinero mañana.*

—*¡Mañana! ¡Siempre (decir) mañana!*

—*Te (dar) mi palabra de honor: mañana tú (ir) a recibir el dinero.*

—*¡Tu palabra de honor! Siempre (prometer), pero nunca (cumplir). Yo no (poder) esperar hasta mañana. A ver. Todavía (tener) el coche, ¿verdad?*

—*Sí. ¿Por qué?*

—*¿Cuánto (valer) el coche?*

—*No (saber). Además, yo no (ir) a vender mi coche. ¡Ni hablar! Ya te he dicho: mañana te (ir) a devolver todo el dinero. ¿No me (creer)?*

—*No, no te (creer).*

—*Pero, ¿por qué no? ¡Yo (ser) tu hermano!*

—*Por eso. Te (conocer) muy bien.*

Practice (3): Knowing the first person singular of certain verbs

There are ten verbs hidden in the word square opposite. All the verbs are in the first person singular form of the Present Tense. Once you have

found them (by looking across or down), use them to complete the ten
sentences on the right.

a	t	c	o	j	o	d	e
b	r	s	v	h	l	i	p
o	a	g	s	a	l	g	o
p	i	v	t	g	i	o	n
e	g	u	e	o	b	s	g
s	o	a	n	d	h	v	o
n	o	i	g	o	p	e	m
c	o	n	o	z	c	o	t

1 ...... *las compras los sábados.*
2 *Siempre* ...... *la verdad.*
3 *No* ...... *durante la semana.*
4 *¿Qué ruido? Yo no* ...... *nada.*
5 ...... *la televisión de vez en cuando.*
6 *Generalmente* ...... *el tren de las siete.*
7 *No la* .... *. ¿Quién es?*
8 *¿Le* ...... *algo, señor?*
9 *¿Dónde* ...... *esta ropa mojada? ¿Allí?*
10 *Lo siento, no* ...... *cambio.*

Practice (4): Building up vocabulary

Below you will find an extract from a Spanish magazine giving details of
a film to be shown on television. Use the following verbs to complete the
extract:

tiene   es   necesita   acepta   soporta   son   abandona   rivalizan   propone

DRAMA

LA LINTERNA ROJA

Intérpretes: Gong Li, Ma Jingwu
Director: Zhang Yimou
China, 1991, Color, 120 min.
Sábado (TVE 1) A las 15.30

Gong Li, una de las actrices más famosas de China, ... *(1) la
protagonista de este drama de mujeres.*
Songlian, una joven de diecinueve años, no .... *(2) vivir con su
madrastra.* .... *(3) la universidad y* .... *(4) la oferta de
matrimonio que le* .... *(5) Chen Zuoquian, un rico que ya* .... *(6)
cincuenta años y tres esposas más. Ahora* .... *(7) cuatro las mujeres
que* .... *(8) por sus favores. Y Soglian* .... *(9) ser más lista que las
demás.*

Extra reference

✦ Some verbs may form the basis of other verbs.

eg *venir* – *con***venir**; *poner* – *su***poner** – *im***poner**; *tener* –
*man***tener** – *con***tener** – *ob***tener**; *coger* – *re***coger** – *es***coger**;
decir – *contra***decir**; *traer* – *at***raer** – *con***traer**.

In such cases you should follow the grammar of the base verbs
when forming these particular verbs.

El horario no me conviene.
The timetable doesn't suit me.

Supongo que sí.
I suppose so.

¿A qué hora te recojo?
What time shall I collect/call for you?

¿No te atraigo?
Don't you find me attractive?

2.2 Using **tener**.

Tienes la piel muy blanca... Tengo ganas de...

While it is relatively easy to recognise and understand the various uses
of **tener** when reading or listening to Spanish, particular problems arise
for English-speakers when trying to use the verb in context. Since **tener**
is such a fundamental verb, you should make absolutely certain that you
are aware of the main areas of difficulty.

● **Using tener to give a description**

Tener is often used to describe appearance (parts of the body or
items of clothing). When **tener** is used in this way, the definite article
(**el, la, los, las**) is usually retained -whereas in English we would not
say 'the'

Tiene **el** *pelo largo.*   = He/she's got long hair.

Tienes **la** *camisa rota.*   = Your shirt is torn.

Tienes **los** *zapatos sucios.* = Your shoes are dirty.
(It is also possible to say: *Tu camisa está rota   Tus zapatos están sucios.*)

● Using **tener** to give general information

When **tener** is followed by a countable noun in a statement which is giving general information, the indefinite article (**un/una**) is not used – whereas in English we would use **a/an**. This also applies to questions and negative statements.

Tengo fiebre.	= I've got a temperature.
Tengo dolor de cabeza.	= I've got a headache.
¿Tiene carnet de conducir?	= Have you got a driving licence?
¿Tiene coche?	= Have you got a car?
No tengo novia.	= I don't have a girlfriend.
No tiene marido.	= She doesn't have a husband.

● Using **tener** to give specific information

On the other hand, **un/una** is used with **tener** – just as in English – when the information becomes much more specific (that is to say, when the question/statement focuses on something that needs to be specified for a particular reason or when **a** really means **one**).

Tengo un hermano y dos hermanas.
I've got a brother and two sisters.

Tengo un coche verde.
I've got a green car.

Tengo un dolor en el pecho.
I've got a pain in my chest. (The focus here is on the word **dolor**.)

¿Tienes una aspirina?
Have you got an aspirin? (*because I need one*)

¿Tienes un boli?
Have you got a biro? (*one that I can use right now*)

● Translating **any**

In English we often use **any** in statements or questions of a general nature. This is not usually necessary in Spanish.

Have you got any friends here?	= *¿Tienes amigos aquí?*
Have you got any experience?	= *¿Tiene experiencia?*
I don't have any money.	= *No tengo dinero.*
I don't have any friends.	= *No tengo amigos.*

I have no idea.   = *No tengo idea.*

However, if the question or statement is slightly more selective or emphatic then **alguno** or **ninguno** may be used.

Do you have any other question? = *¿Tiene alguna otra pregunta?*

Do you have any previous
experience?   = *¿Tiene alguna experiencia previa?*

If you have any doubts....   = *Si tienes alguna duda...*

I don't have any ideas.   = *No tengo ninguna idea.*

● **Tener = to have or to be?**

A particular problem for English-speaking students is that in English we have many expressions that follow the pattern of 'to be + (very) + adjective', whereas in Spanish the pattern is **tener + (mucho) + noun**. The following list should be learnt by heart:

tener .... años	= to be .... years old
tener (mucho) frío	= to be (very) cold (*referring to people*)
tener (mucho) calor	= to be (very) hot (*referring to people*)
tener (mucha) hambre	= to be (very) hungry
tener éxito	= to be successful
tener (mucha) suerte	= to be (very) lucky
tener prisa	= to be in a hurry
tener razón	= to be right
tener sueño	= to be/feel sleepy
tener miedo (de)	= to be afraid (of)
tener cuidado	= to be careful
tener gracia	= to be amusing/funny
tener celos	= to be jealous
tener la culpa	= to be one's fault
tener vergüenza	= to be/feel ashamed

● **Using tener to express obligation**

Do not forget that **tener + que + infinitive** means 'to have to do' (obligation/necessity).

Tengo que volver a Londres lo antes posible.
I have to return to London as soon as possible.

- Note, too, that 'to have something to do' is translated by **tener algo que hacer.**

  ¿Tiene algo que declarar?
  Do you have anything to declare?

  Esto no tiene nada que ver con el asunto.
  This has got nothing to do with the matter at hand.

- Idiomatic expressions with **tener**

  Pay particular attention to idiomatic phrases with **tener.** There are many of them! Here is just a brief selection:

Tengo ganas de ver esa película.	=	I fancy seeing that film.
¿Tiene fuego?	=	Have you got a light?
¿Tiene hora?	=	Have you got the time?
Tenga la bondad de acompañarme.	=	Would you please come with me.
¿Qué tiene José?	=	What's up/the matter with José?

Practice (5): Recognising and using basic phrases with tener

On the left are ten different people speaking. On the right are ten people replying. Match each speaker in column 1 with a speaker from column 2.

Speakers 1

1 —*Quisiera hablar con el director.*

2 —*¿En qué puedo servirle a usted?*

3 —*¿Tiene jamón?*

4 —*¿Por qué no te gusta este hotel?*

5 —*¿Tiene una habitación individual?*

6 —*¿Tiene baño la habitación?*

7 —*¿Qué hora tienes?*

8 —*¿Por qué estás en casa?*

9 —*Aquí tiene.*

10 —*¿Tenemos leche?*

Speakers 2

a —*¿Serrano o york?*

b —*No tiene piscina.*

c —*¿Tiene usted cita?*

d —*Hoy no tenemos clase.*

e —*Sí, pero no tenemos azúcar.*

f —*Gracias.*

g —*¿Tiene corbatas de seda?*

h —*No, pero tiene ducha.*

i —*¿Para cuántas noches?*

j —*No sé, no llevo reloj.*

Practice (6): Recognising translation problems with **tener**

Select the most appropriate translation.

1) Do you have a boyfriend? (*general question*)
    a *¿Tienes un novio?*
    b *¿Tienes novio?*

2) Have you got a torch? (*because I need one*)
    a *¿Tienes una linterna?*
    b *¿Tienes linterna?*

3) Have you got a map of this region?
    a *¿Tiene un mapa de esta región?*
    b *¿Tiene mapa de esta región?*

4) Have you got a video-recorder? (*general question*)
    a *¿Tienes un vídeo?*
    b *¿Tienes vídeo?*

5) We don't have a washing-machine.
    a *No tenemos una lavadora.*
    b *No tenemos lavadora.*

6) Have you got any change?
    a *¿Tiene algún cambio?*
    b *¿Tiene cambio?*

7) We haven't got any eggs.
    a *No tenemos algunos huevos.*
    b *No tenemos huevos.*

8) I haven't got any stamps.
    a *No tengo algunos sellos.*
    b *No tengo sellos.*

9) Have you got any coffee?
    a *¿Tienes café?*
    b *¿Tienes algún café?*

10) Have you got any news (at all)?
    a *¿Tienes noticia?*
    b *¿Tienes alguna noticia?*

Practice (7): Forming phrases with **tener**

Use the following words to complete the questions or statements below.

razón   culpa   años   suerte   frío   frías   éxito   mucho   mucha   sueño
ganas   miedo   tiene   nada   gracia   el   prisa   que

  1 *Tienes las manos .... ¿Estás bien?*

  2 *Tengo .... ¿Ponemos la calefacción?*

  3 *No tengo .... hambre, pero comeré algo.*

  4 *Tengo ....calor. Voy a quitarme la chaqueta.*

  5 *No puedes salir así: tienes .... abrigo sucio.*

  6 *Para tener ...., hay que ser positivo.*

  7 *Tengo .... Voy a acostarme.*

  8 *No tengo .... de salir. ¿Por qué no nos quedamos en casa?*

  9 *¿Tienes .... de los perros?*

10 *No, no tienes .... Estás completamente equivocado.*

11 *No hay problema; yo puedo esperar. No tengo ....*

12 *Tenemos .... hacerlo ahora mismo.*

13 *¿Por qué se ríe la gente? Para mí, no tiene ninguna ....*

14 *Tengo veintiún ...., igual que mi novio, Carlos.*

15 *Y, ¿por qué me gritas a mí? Yo no tengo la ....*

16 *No tengo .... que decir. Quiero ver a mi abogado.*

17 *¿Qué .... Alicia? ¿Le pasa algo?*

18 *Es el tercer premio que has ganado. ¡Qué .... tienes!*

Extra reference

Note the following construction:

✦ *Tiene que haber alguien allí, porque la luz está encendida.*
   There has to be/must be somebody there because the light is on.

✦ Here are a few more useful phrases with **tener**:

tener lugar	= to take place
tener en cuenta	= to take into account/bear in mind
tener sentido	= to make sense

2.3 Forming and using reflexive verbs.

me voy a bañar   te vas a poner como un cangrejo si no te
proteges la piel   tengo ganas de meterme en el agua
se pelea   se ahoga

● A verb becomes reflexive in the following way:

Normal: *llamar* (to call)	**Reflexive**: *llamarse* (to be called)
(yo) llamo	*(yo) me llamo*
(tú) llamas	*(tú) te llamas*
(él,ella,Vd) llama	*(él,ella,Vd) se llama*
(nosotros/as) llamamos	*(nosotros/as) nos llamamos*
(vosotros/as) llamáis	*(vosotros/as) os llamáis*
(ellos/as,Vds) llaman	*(ellos/as,Vds) se llaman*

● **The Infinitive + reflexive pronoun**

With an infinitive construction, the reflexive pronoun is either kept
with the verb or placed right in front of the construction.

(Yo) voy a bañarme. (Yo) me voy a bañar.
I'm going for a swim.

¿Vas a ponerte el vestido nuevo? ¿Te vas a poner el vestido nuevo?
Are you going to put on your new dress?

● The purpose of the reflexive pronoun

There are various reasons why a verb becomes reflexive:

a) To emphasise that an action is happening to **self** rather than to
something or somebody else.

Lavo el coche.   = I wash the car.

Me lavo.   = I wash myself.

b) To distinguish between description and action (change of state).

estar sentado (to be sitting) *sentarse* (to sit down)

estar borracho (to be drunk) *emborracharse* (to get drunk)

estar enfadado (to be angry) *enfadarse* (to get angry)

c) Most verbs that usually take an object become reflexive if they are used without an object.

¿Quieres cerrar la puerta?
Would you close the door, please? (The door is the object of the verb 'close'.)

¿A qué hora se cierra el supermercado?
At what time does the supermarket close? (In this case, there is no object following the verb 'close'.)

d) When an active verb is used with parts of the body or items of clothing, it usually becomes reflexive.

Me cepillo los dientes antes de acostarme.
I brush my teeth before going to bed.

¿Por qué no te pones los guantes?
Why don't you put on your gloves?

Voy a quitarme la chaqueta.
I'm going to take off my jacket. (This rule does not apply to such descriptive verbs as **tener, llevar** and **doler**.)

f) Sometimes a verb has a different meaning when it is made reflexive.

Se pone triste. = He/she becomes sad.

Se hace tarde. = It's getting late.

● **The special function of se**

Apart from its normal function as a reflexive pronoun, **se** has another extremely important function. You should pay particular attention to the way **se** (+ the third person singular/plural of a verb) is used to form an impersonal/neutral construction. This impersonal construction is used in the following ways:

a) It is used instead of the passive. This is very important because, wherever possible, the passive is avoided in Spanish. Look very carefully at the following examples:

Se produce vino en esta región. = Wine is produced in this region.

Se cultivan naranjas aquí. = Oranges are grown here.

Se vende pan en una panadería. = Bread is sold in a baker's.

Se habla español en Ecuador. = Spanish is spoken in Ecuador.

b) It is used to make general statements or questions (where in English we might use 'they' or 'people').

¿A qué hora se cena en España?
At what time do people have dinner in Spain?

Se bebe mucho vino en España.
They drink a lot of wine in Spain.

c) It is used to make general statements or questions (where in English we might use 'one' or 'you').

¿Dónde se puede aparcar?
Where can one park?

¿Cómo se llega a la catedral?
How do you/does one get to the cathedral?

Practice (8): Understanding the function and use of reflexive verbs

For each pair of sentences, write in the correct form of the verb that is given. In each case, one of the sentences will contain a reflexive verb.

1) esconder

    a *Mi hermano menor siempre ...... detrás del sofá cuando hay visita.*

    b *Mi hermano menor siempre ...... sus juguetes cuando nuestros primos vienen a visitarnos.*

2) enojar

    a *Cuando mi tío se emborracha, se pone pesado y ...... a todo el mundo.*

    b *Mi tía ...... cuando mi tío se emborracha.*

3) cuidar

    a *Miguel trabaja en un parque zoológico. Él ...... de los animales.*

    b *Miguel no .... Fuma demasiado, no come bien y nunca hace ejercicio.*

4) cortar

    a *Tienes que ...... el pelo.*

    b *Tienes que tener cuidado cuando ...... esta tela.*

5) cenar

    a *¿A qué hora ...... ustedes?*

    b *¿A qué hora ...... en España?*

6) comer

    a *Tú ...... demasiados dulces.*

    b *Dicen que ...... bien en aquel restaurante.*

7 bañar

　　a *¿Queréis ...... ?*

　　b *Por las tardes yo ...... a los niños mientras mi esposa prepara la cena.*

8 necesitar

　　a *Los animales y las plantas ...... mutuamente.*

　　b *El hombre también ...... a los animales y las plantas.*

Practice (9): Avoiding the passive with se

Complete the passage below with the following verbs:

se ponen　se llevan　se clasifican　se mezcla　se les quita　se recogen　se necesitan

EL CHOCOLATE

Para hacer chocolate .... granos de cacao y azúcar.
El cacao es un árbol tropical cuyo fruto tiene forma de balón de rugby. Las semillas que hay en su interior son parecidas a almendras, con cáscara y todo. Cuando llega la época de la recolección, ... los frutos maduros y se les sacan las semillas, ... éstas al sol para que se sequen, ... y limpian y por fin se tuestan. Luego .... la cáscara con unas máquinas especiales y los granos tostados .... a moler. Una vez molido, el cacao .... con azúcar en un recipiente y se calienta hasta obtener una pasta muy líquida. Esta pasta, vertida en moldes adecuados y enfriada, es el chocolate.

Practice (10): Recognising when to use se + verb

Underline the correct form of the verbs in brackets. If the verb is passive in meaning (is done/are done), it will take **se**. The first one has been done for you as an example.

　　eg　*Cómo (hace, se hace) la mantequilla*

La mantequilla (saca, se saca) de la leche. En la leche hay miles de partículas de grasa que, reunidas, (forman, se forman) la mantequilla. En las fábricas, la crema de la leche (deposita, se deposita) en unos recipientes que (parecen, se parecen) enormes tambores. Al girar éstos, (bate, se bate) la crema. Entonces, las partículas de grasa (unen, se unen) y (forman, se forman) copos de mantequilla que, a su vez, (juntan, se juntan) en una gran masa. El resto de la crema, la parte que no (transforma, se transforma) en mantequilla, (saca, se saca) del tambor. Es lo que (llama, se llama) suero de manteca.

Extra reference

✦ A reflexive verb does not just convey the idea of 'self/selves'. It can also convey the idea of 'each other'.

Se miraron pero no se saludaron.
They looked at each other, but they did not greet each other.

Nos ayudamos.
We help(ed) each other.

To avoid ambiguity, it may sometimes be necessary to add an extra phrase to show more clearly who the reflexive pronoun is referring to:

Se miraron el uno al otro.	= They looked at each other.
Se miraron la una a la otra.	= They looked at each other.
Se miraron unos a otros.	= They looked at one another.

Equally, it may sometimes be necessary to add an extra phrase to show that **se** refers to **selves** and not to **each other**.

Se están engañando a sí mismos.
They are fooling/deceiving themselves.

✦ In spoken Spanish, verbs are often made reflexive in order to give emphasis and/or to give the idea of completion.

—*Se lo comió todo.*	= He ate it all.
—*No me lo creo.*	= I just don't believe it.
—*No me lo puedo creer.*	= I just can't believe it.

✦ Here are some useful reflexive verbs that are well worth learning by heart:

ponerse a + infinitive	= to begin doing something
encogerse de hombros	= to shrug one's shoulders
darse cuenta (de que)	= to realise (that)
quejarse (de)	= to complain (about)
irse/marcharse	= to leave/go away
irse a la cama	= to go to bed

Progress test 2

Translate the following items into Spanish.

1 You don't smoke, do you?

2 I bring; I can; I make; I see; I hear; I say; I go out; I come; I take (*coger*); I know (*saber*); I know (*conocer*).

3 We give; we sell; we can; we want; we have; we open; we suffer.

4 Your trousers are dirty.

5 She has blue eyes.

6 He's got a headache.

7 I don't have any money.

8 I am not very hungry.

9 I feel very sleepy.

10 We are not in a hurry.

11 We don't have anything to declare.

12 He never gets angry.

13 What times does the bank open?

14 Why don't you take off your jacket?

15 English is spoken here.

UNIT 3 Exchanging information

Enrique has arranged to meet his girlfriend in a bar. When he goes in, he sees an old friend.

Enrique: ¡Hombre! ¡Pedro! <u>Hace mucho que no te veo.</u> ¿Cómo 3.1
anda tu vida?

Pedro: Pues, regular. Y tú ¿qué tal?

Enrique: Muy bien. Todo va muy bien.

Pedro: Y, ¿cómo está Teresa?

Enrique: Ya no salgo con ella. Tengo otra novia. Se llama
Consuelo. <u>Salgo con ella desde hace tres meses.</u> Es 3.1
una chica divina. Tengo mucha suerte. Y tú ¿qué?
¿<u>Sigues</u> con Lola? 3.5

Pedro: Sí.

Enrique: Y, ¿qué tal el trabajo? ¿Sigues trabajando en la
misma oficina?

Pedro: Sí, pero <u>pienso</u> cambiar de trabajo. 3.5

Enrique: ¿Por qué?

Pedro: <u>Llevo más de cinco años trabajando allí,</u> pero no 3.1
estoy contento. <u>Siempre hago lo mismo.</u> La rutina 3.4
no cambia. El trabajo es pesado y no quieren

subirme el sueldo. Además, es una jornada muy
larga. <u>Empiezo</u> sobre las ocho y a veces no termino   3.5
hasta las ocho de la noche. En fin, <u>me siento</u>   3.5
bastante frustrado.

Enrique: ¿<u>Sabes utilizar</u> un procesador de textos?   3.2

Pedro: Sí, por supuesto. ¿Por qué?

Enrique: Pues, el padre de mi novia tiene una empresa
bastante grande y, según Consuelo, <u>les hace falta</u>   3.3
ayuda en la oficina. ¿Te interesa?

Pedro: Pues sí, pero <u>no puedo empezar</u> inmediatamente.   3.2
Tendré que avisarle a mi jefe lo menos con dos
semanas de anticipación.

Enrique: Vale. Mira, aquí viene Consuelo. Te voy a presentar.
<u>Podemos hablar</u> con ella a ver si....¿Qué pasa? ¿Por   3.2
qué frunces el ceño? ¿<u>La conoces?</u>   3.2

Pedro: <u>Sí, la conozco.</u> ¡Es la hija de mi jefe!   3.2

3.1 Practising time expressions

**hace mucho que no te veo   salgo con ella desde hace tres
meses   llevo más de cinco años trabajando allí**

● Certain time expressions in Spanish are radically different from their
equivalent in English. This can lead to some confusion, and so these
expressions should be learnt very carefully. The important point to
note is that where in English we use the Present Perfect ('I have
done') in certain time expressions, the Spanish prefer the Present
Tense or the Present Continuous.

● **Using llevar in time constructions**

In spoken Spanish, perhaps the most natural time construction is
that with **llevar**. Study carefully the following patterns, paying
particular attention to the examples in the negative:

a) *¿Cuánto tiempo lleva ella en el extranjero?*
How long has she been abroad?

Ella lleva tres años en el extranjero.
She has been abroad for three years.

b) *¿Cuánto tiempo llevan trabajando allí?*
How long have they been working there?

¿Llevan mucho tiempo trabajando allí?
Have they been working there long?

Llevan cuatro años trabajando allí.
They have been working there for four years.

c) *María lleva seis meses sin ver a su familia.*
María has not seen her family for six months.

Pedro lleva tres semanas sin fumar un cigarrillo.
Pedro hasn't smoked a cigarette for three weeks.

● **Using desde hace in time constructions**

Equally common, though perhaps slightly more formal, is the time construction with **desde hace** (for). Study carefully the following patterns:

a) *¿Desde hace cuánto (tiempo) la conoces?*
How long have you known her (for)?

La conozco desde hace diez años.
I have known her for ten years.

b) *¿Desde hace cuánto (tiempo) están esperando?*
How long have they been waiting (for)?

Están esperando desde hace media hora.
They have been waiting for half an hour.

c) NB: In the negative, it is possible to use either the Present Tense or the Present Perfect.

No bebe alcohol desde hace cuatro meses.
No ha bebido alcohol desde hace cuatro meses.
He hasn't drunk any alcohol for four months.

● **Using hace ... que in time constructions**

The third way of forming a time construction is to use **hace ... que**. Study carefully the following patterns:

a) *¿Hace cuánto tiempo que trabaja usted allí?*
How long have you worked there?

Hace diez años que trabajo allí.
I have worked there for ten years.

b) *¿Hace mucho (tiempo) que eres profesor?*
Have you been a teacher for long?

Hace quince años que soy profesor.
I have been a teacher for fifteen years.

c) *Hace mucho que no te veo.*
I haven't seen you for a long time.
(It is also possible to say, *Hace mucho que no te he visto.*)

Practice (1): Forming time constructions

a) Using **llevar**, translate the following items:
    1 How long have we been waiting for the bus?
    2 Have you (*tú*) been here long?
    3 I haven't eaten meat for nearly two years.
    4 He hasn't worked for over three years.

b) Using **desde hace**, translate the following items:
    1 How long have they lived in Valladolid?
    2 They have lived in Segovia for six years.
    3 I have had this car for three months.
    4 We have been friends for fifteen years.
    5 I haven't smoked for nine months.

c) Using **hace ... que** translate the following items:
    1 Have they been here long?
    2 I haven't been to the theatre for a long time. (use *ir*)
    3 I haven't seen her for ten years.

Extra reference

✦ **acabar de + infinitive**

'To have just done something' is translated by the Present Tense of
acabar + infinitive. Study the following examples very carefully:

El avión acaba de aterrizar.
The plane has just landed.

Acabo de escribir una carta.
I have just written a letter.

Acabamos de empezar.
We have just begun.

3.2 Using **saber, poder** and **conocer.**

¿Sabes utilizar...?   No puedo empezar...   Podemos hablar...
¿La conoces?   Sí, la conozco.

● **Conocer or saber?**

Both **conocer** and **saber** can be translated as **to know.** The difference between the two verbs is as follows:

- To know a person or a place = **conocer.**
  ¿Conoce usted España?
  Do you know Spain?
  No conozco a su marido.
  I don't know her husband.

- To know a concrete fact = **saber**
  Necesito saber unos datos personales.
  I need to know some personal details.
  No saben nada.
  They don't know anything.

- To know + (in)direct speech = **saber.**
  No sé dónde está.
  I don't know where he is.
  Yo sé que tú estás cansado.
  I know that you are tired.

● **Saber or poder?**

Both **saber** and **poder** can be translated as **can.** The difference between the two verbs is as follows:

- When 'can' means 'know how to' (the focus being on a specific ability or skill), then you must use **saber.** Any statement or question using **saber** in this way will be a very general one.
  ¿Sabe usted conducir?
  Can you drive?
  ¿Sabes utilizar un procesador de textos?
  Can you use a word-processor?
  No sé nadar.
  I can't swim. (*I haven't learnt to swim.*)

- When the focus of **can** is on specific possibility (*is it possible or not?*), then you should use **poder**.

  ¿Cuándo puedes empezar?
  When can you start? (*When is it possible for you to start?*)
  No puedo hacerlo.
  I can't do it. (*For some reason or other, it's not possible for me to do it.*)

Practice (2): Distinguishing between **conocer** and **saber**

Using the Present Tense of either **conocer** or **saber**, complete the gaps below.

1 *No, yo no .... Portugal. Nunca he estado allí.*

2 *—¿...... usted algún restaurante bueno por aquí?*
   —No, lo siento, es que no .... este barrio. Pero yo .... dónde hay un restaurante muy bueno. ¿........ usted la calle de San Juan cerca de la Plaza Mayor?
   —Sí, yo .... dónde queda esa calle.

3 *—¿........ usted a María Ramos?*
   —Sí, la .... desde hace mucho tiempo.

4 *Ella está desesperada. Ella no .... qué hacer.*

5 *Nosotros .... la verdad desde hace seis meses.*

6 *Mi tío .... mucho: es muy inteligente.*

Practice (3): Distinguishing between **saber** and **poder**

Use **sabes** or **puedes** to complete each question below.

1 *¿........ tocar el piano? (general question)*

2 *¿........ venir esta noche?*

3 *¿........ prestarme mil pesetas?*

4 *¿........ esquiar? (general question)*

5 *¿........ hacerme un favor?*

6 *¿........ trabajar este domingo?*

7 *¿........ jugar al ajedrez? (general question)*

8 *¿........ nadar? (general question)*

9 *¿........ leer? (general question)*

10 *¿........ leer lo que he escrito?*

Extra reference

✦ Be very careful when translating 'can/can't hear' or 'can/can't see' into Spanish. Look carefully at the following examples:

No puedo oír.   = I can't hear. (*I am deaf.*)

No oigo (nada).   = I can't hear (anything). (*There's no sound.*)

No puedo ver.   = I can't see. (*I am blind.*)

No veo (nada)   = I can't see (anything). (*It's too dark for me to see.*)

NB: If 'can' means 'may' (permission), then there is no problem of usage:

¿Puedo ver el programa?
Can/may I see the programme?

✦ Note the following idiomatic phrase:

No puedo más.   = I've had enough. / I can't take any more. I'm shattered. / I'm exhausted.

✦ When **saber** is used on its own, it is usual to place **lo** in front:

Yo lo sé.   = I know.

No lo sé.   = I don't know.

In spoken Spanish, **ya** is often placed in front of **lo** and **saber** as a form of emphasis.

Ya lo sé.   = I know (that).

✦ Note the following use of **saber + algo/nada + de**:

¿Sabes algo de Antonio? = Any news of Antonio?

No sé nada de él. = I haven't heard from him. / I don't know what's been happening with him – I haven't heard anything.

¡No quiero saber nada de él! = Don't mention his name! / I don't want to know anything about him!

3.3 Recognising the various uses of **hacer**.

les hace falta ayuda

● Like **tener, hacer** is a very versatile verb which is used in a variety of contexts. We saw in the first section (3.1) of this unit, for example, how **hace ... que** and **desde hace** are used in time expressions.

● **Hacer** has two basic meanings: **do** and **make**.

hacer la compra	= to do the shopping
hacer un favor	= to do a favour
hacer un esfuerzo	= to make an effort
hacer un viaje	= to make a journey

● **Using hacer to describe weather conditions**

As you will already know, **hacer** is used impersonally in many weather expressions. There are two points to remember when forming weather expressions:

i) If you want to say 'very' or 'so' hot/cold/sunny, you must use **mucho** for **very** and **tanto** for **so**.

Hace (mucho) sol.	= It is (very) sunny.
Hace (mucho/tanto) calor.	= It is (very/so) hot.
Hace (mucho/tanto) frío.	= It is (very/so) cold.

ii) Be careful when using **malo** and **bueno**. These words drop the **o** in front of a masculine noun (eg 'tiempo').

Hace un tiempo muy bueno. Hace bueno. Hace malo.
but *Hace buen tiempo. Hace mal tiempo.*

Note the following expression:

Hace un día espléndido. = It's a lovely/marvellous day.

● **Hacer falta**

Another example of an impersonal construction is **hacer falta** (to need/to be needed). When used with a person, **hacer falta** has the same indirect pattern as **gustar**.

Hace falta mucho dinero. = A lot of money is needed.

Me hace falta dinero.   = I need money.

Les hace falta ayuda.   = They need (some) help.

● **Hacer + infinitive + noun**

Note very carefully the word order in Spanish when **hacer** is used with a noun and an infinitive.

hacer construir una casa = to have a house built

hacer esperar a alguien   = to make someone wait

● **Hacer may be translated in a variety of ways**

In the following phrases, note the translation of **hacer**.

hacer cola   = to form a queue/to stand in line

hacer la maleta   = to pack a suitcase

hacer caso (a)   = to take notice (of)/to pay attention (to)

hacer una pregunta   = to ask a question

hacer una visita   = to pay a visit

● **Idioms with hacer**

There are many idiomatic phrases with hacer. Look carefully at the examples below, paying particular attention to the phrases with **hacerse**.

no hacer más que
   (+ infinitive)   = to do nothing but...

hacer el ridículo   = to make a fool of oneself

Deja de hacer el tonto.
¡Estás haciendo el ridículo!

hacer el tonto	=	to act like a fool
hacer la vista gorda	=	to turn a blind eye / to look the other way
hacer daño a	=	to harm
hacerse daño	=	to get hurt / to hurt oneself
hacerse a la mar	=	to put out to sea
hacerse amigo de	=	to make friends with
hacerse amigos	=	to become friends
hacerse médico	=	to become a doctor
hacerse tarde	=	to get/grow late

Practice (4): Forming phrases with **hacer**

Choose the most appropriate alternative to complete each sentence.

1) *No sé qué hacer con mi hija. Ella nunca me hace* ....
   a *atención*
   b *caso*
   c *respeto*

2) *No es como antes. La gente ya no hace* .... *en las paradas de autobús.*
   a *cola*
   b *fila*
   c *línea*

3) —*¿Le ayudo?*
   —*Es usted muy amable, pero no hace* .... *Gracias de todas maneras.*
   a *necesario*
   b *falta*
   c *necesidad*

4) *Lo que* .... *hace falta es una botella de vino.*
   a *nosotros*
   b *a nosotros*
   c *nos*

5) *¡Cuidado! Puedes hacerte* ....
   a *dolor*
   b *daño*
   c *herido*

6) *¿Dónde está Manolo? ¡Siempre nos hace ....*
   a *espera*
   b *esperando*
   c *esperar*

7) *¡No aguanto más! Voy a hacer .... y me voy a marchar.*
   a *las maletas*
   b *la cama*
   c *la ropa*

8) *Pedro es muy pesado. No hace .... criticar.*
   a *sólo*
   b *más que*
   c *nada*

9) *No hace .... frío hoy, ¿verdad?*
   a *tan*
   b *muy*
   c *tanto*

10) *¡Menos mal que el guardia hizo la vista .... !*
   a *ciega*
   b *gorda*
   c *contraria*

11) *¡Date prisa! Se está haciendo ....*
   a *el tonto*
   b *tarde*
   c *calor*

12) *Quiero .... amigo de aquel chico.*
   a *hacer*
   b *hacerse*
   c *hacerme*

Extra reference

Try not to confuse **hacer un favor** (to do a favour) with **hacer el favor de + infinitive** (a phrase used when making a request).

   ¿Me haces un gran favor?   = Can you do me a great favour?

   Haga el favor de firmar aquí. = Would you please sign here.

3.4 Using **lo + adjective**.

Siempre hago lo mismo

● In English we often make such statements as 'I think the same', 'The best thing is …', 'The only thing that …', or 'The good thing is that…'. In Spanish such neutral phrases are translated by **lo + masculine adjective**.

Pienso lo mismo.	=	I think the same.
Lo mejor es …	=	The best thing is …
Lo único que …	=	The only thing that …
Lo bueno es que …	=	The good thing is that …

● Note that **que** usually follows **lo mismo** if a comparison is being made.

Piensan lo mismo que nosotros.	= They think they same as us/we do.
Hago lo mismo que ellos.	= I do the same as them/they do.

However, **de** is used with **siempre**.

Lo mismo de siempre.	= The same as usual/ever/always.

Practice (5): Recognising and using basic phrases with **lo**

Form eight complete sentences by matching items 1–8 with items a–h.

1 *Y lo mejor de todo es que*

2 *Lo único que quiero*

3 *Lo malo es que tenemos*

4 *Lo primero que tienes que aprender es*

5 *Lo mejor que puedes hacer*

6 *Lo peor que puedes*

7 *Lo principal es*

8 *Lo más importante es no*

a   *es callarte.*

b   *perder la fe.*

c   *es estar a tu lado.*

d   *encontrar suficiente dinero.*

e   *que empezar de nuevo.*

f   *a tener más paciencia.*

g   *me van a subir el sueldo.*

h   *hacer en este momento es hablar con él.*

Extra reference

✦ **Lo + adjective** can also mean **how** when it follows such verbs as **saber, ver, darse cuenta, imaginarse** and **comprender**. In this construction the adjective can be masculine or feminine and is always followed by **que**. Look carefully at the following examples:

> *No te puedes imaginar lo duro que es mi trabajo.*
> You cannot imagine how hard my job/work is.

> *No tienes idea de lo difícil que es.*
> You have no idea how difficult it is.

> *No se dan cuenta de lo importante que es.*
> They don't realise how important it is.

✦ Developing vocabulary

The following phrases with **lo** should be learnt by heart:

por lo menos	= at least
a lo mejor	= probably, maybe, with any luck
por lo visto	= apparently
a lo lejos	= in the distance
a lo largo de	= along
lo antes posible	= as soon as possible
en lo alto de una montaña	= on the top of a mountain

3.5. Forming and using radical-changing verbs

sigues   pienso   empiezo   me siento

- The formation of **radical-changing** verbs (present indicative)

  There are three rules you need to learn in order to be able to form the present tense of radical-changing verbs

  Rule 1: -AR and -ER radical-changing verbs.

  When stressed, **e** becomes **ie** and **o** becomes **ue**. The first and second persons plural do not change because the stress does not fall on the **e** or the **o**.

  empezar (to begin):
  empiezo, empiezas, empieza, empezamos, empezáis, empiezan.

  perder (to lose):
  pierdo, pierdes, pierde, perdemos, perdéis, pierden.

  contar (to count):
  cuento, cuentas, cuenta, contamos, contáis, cuentan.

  volver (to return):
  vuelvo, vuelves, vuelve, volvemos, volvéis, vuelven.

  The most common verbs in this category are:
  acordarse (to remember); *acostarse* (to go to bed); *almorzar* (to have lunch); *cerrar* (to shut); *colgar* (to hang); *costar* (to cost); *doler* (to hurt); *despertarse* (to wake up); *encontrar* (to find); *entender* (to understand); *llover* (to rain); *mover* (to move); *mostrar* (to show); *nevar* (to snow); *pensar* (to think); *soler* (to tend to); *sentarse* (to sit down); *sonar* (to ring); *soñar* (to dream); *volar* (to fly).

  Note also the verb *jugar* (to play):
  juego, juegas, juega, jugamos, jugáis, juegan.

  Rule 2: -IR radical-changing verbs (group 1).

  Certain -IR verbs change in the same way as -AR and -ER verbs. When stressed, **e** becomes **ie** and **o** becomes **ue**.

  preferir (to prefer):
  prefiero, prefieres, prefiere, preferimos, preferís, prefieren.

  dormir (to sleep):
  duermo, duermes, duerme, dormimos, dormís, duermen.

Other verbs in this category include:
advertir (to notice/warn); *divertirse* (to enjoy oneself); *mentir* (to tell lies); *morir* (to die); *referir* (to refer); *sentir*(se) (to feel).

Rule 3: -IR radical-changing verbs (group 2).
With certain IR verbs, **e** changes to **i** when stressed.

pedir (to ask for):
pido, pides, pide, pedimos, pedís, piden.

servir (to serve) :
sirvo, sirves, sirve, servimos, servís, sirven.

seguir (to follow):
sigo, sigues, sigue, seguimos, seguís, siguen.

Other verbs in this category include:
conseguir (to get/obtain); *corregir* (to correct); *elegir* (to choose); *medir* (to measure); *reírse* (to laugh); *reñir* (to quarrel/scold); *repetir* (to repeat); *sonreír* (to smile); *vestirse* (to get dressed).

Practice (6): Becoming familiar with common radical-changing verbs

Complete the following dialogue by changing each verb in brackets into the correct form of the Present Tense.

—*Cada vez que te (pedir) un favor, tú (negarse) a ayudarme. Tú (encontrar) cualquier pretexto para no complacerme. Si tú (seguir) así, voy a pedir un divorcio. Ya no aguanto más.*
—*Pero, es que no (encontrarse) bien. De verdad, yo (sentirse) mal.*
—*¿Qué te pasa esta vez?*
—*Me (doler) el estómago.*
—*¿Por qué no (acostarse)?*
—*Primero (querer) ir a la farmacia a comprar algo para quitarme el dolor.*
—*Son las ocho y media de la noche. Si yo (acordarse) bien, la farmacia (cerrarse) a las seis.*
—*Voy de todas maneras a ver si está abierta.*
—*Pero aquí hay medicinas. Mira. ¿No te (servir) esta medicina?*
—*No, me hace falta algo más fuerte.*
—*Como ocho cañas de cerveza, me imagino.*
—*Me voy, hasta luego.*
—*Y ¿a qué hora (pensar) volver?*
—*Pronto, mi amor.*
—*Si tú (volver) a casa borracho, te lo juro, yo....*
—*Pero tú no (entender) mi punto de vista, cariño.*

—*De verdad, Antonio, tú me sacas de quicio.*
—*Hasta la vista, mi vida.*

Practice (7): Building up useful expressions with radical-changing verbs

Match items 1–6 with items a–f. Change each verb in brackets into the correct form of the Present Tense.

1 *Me (costar) mucho trabajo*

2 *Mi hermana (soñar) con*

3 *Y tú ¿qué (soler)*

4 *José y yo estamos separados*

5 *Las Autoridades Sanitarias (advertir) que*

6 *La ballena azul es tan larga como ocho elefantes en fila.*

a *hacer los sábados?*

b *(Medir) aproximadamente treinta metros de largo.*

c *el tabaco perjudica seriamente la salud.*

d *ser actriz y modelo.*

e *levantarme por las mañanas.*

f *pero (seguir) siendo amigos.*

Extra reference

✦ Developing vocabulary

Note carefully the verb patterns with the following radical-changing verbs:

pensar hacer algo	= to intend to do something/ to think of doing something.
soñar con hacer algo	= to dream of doing something.
negarse a hacer algo	= to refuse to do something.
seguir haciendo algo	= to carry on/continue doing something.
volver a hacer algo	= to do something again.
soler hacer algo	= to usually do something.
empezar a hacer algo	= to begin doing/to do something.

Progress test 3

Translate the following into Spanish.

1 How long have they been waiting? (Use **llevar**)
2 I have known Pedro for two years. (Use **desde hace**)
3 I haven't seen you for a long time. (Use **hace ... que**)
4 They have just arrived.
5 Can you play the guitar? (*general question*)
6 I know the truth.
7 They need money. (Use **hacer falta**)
8 It's so hot here.
9 Can I ask a question?
10 She takes no notice of her mother.
11 He always makes a fool of himself.
12 The good thing is that we don't have to pay.
13 I begin; I lose; I return; I prefer; I sleep; it snows; it rains.
14 He doesn't feel very well.
15 What are you thinking of doing?

UNIT 4 Establishing what is happening and what has happened

Luis has just entered his flat after a hard day at work, and his wife greets him.

Isabel: Hola, querido. <u>La merienda está lista.</u> ¿Qué tal el día?   4.1

Luis: ¡Ni lo preguntes!

Isabel: <u>Estás temblando,</u> mi amor. ¿Te pasa algo?   4.1/4.3

Luis: No me pasa nada. Voy a ducharme.

Isabel: <u>Estás de mal humor,</u> ¿verdad? Se te nota en la voz y en la cara. <u>¿Cuál es el problema?</u>   4.1 4.2

Luis: ¡No hay ningún problema!

Isabel: Algo pasa.

Luis: ¡No pasa nada!

Isabel: ¿Cómo que nada? <u>Algo te está fastidiando.</u> ¿Qué <u>ha sucedido? ¿He hecho yo algo?</u>   4.4; 4.2/4.5 4.5

Luis: <u>Te he dicho</u> que no es nada.   4.5

Isabel: Entonces, ¿por qué me estás gritando?

Luis:	¡No te estoy gritando! ¿Es que no puedo levantar la voz de vez en cuando? Y ahora, ¿por qué estás llorando?	4.4; 4.6 4.3

Luis: ¡No te estoy gritando! ¿Es que no puedo levantar 4.4; 4.6
la voz de vez en cuando? Y ahora, ¿por qué estás 4.3
llorando?

Isabel: Tú sabes que no me gusta pelear contigo.

Luis: ¡Pero no estamos peleando!   4.3

Isabel: ¿Ves? Ahora mismo me estás gritando. ¿Qué es   4.3; 4.2
lo que pasa?

Luis: Discúlpame, mi amor. No es culpa tuya. Es que   4.1
he recibido una noticia muy mala.   4.5

Isabel: ¿Qué noticia? ¿Qué ha ocurrido?   4.2; 4.5

Luis: Me han despedido.   4.5

Isabel: Pero, ¿por qué? Llevas más de veinte años
trabajando allí. Te llevas bien con el jefe. Tú eres 4.1
buen trabajador. ¿Por qué te han despedido?

Luis: La empresa ha perdido mucho dinero en los   4.5
últimos dos años. Para ellos, sale más barato
emplear a los jóvenes que a los viejos.

Isabel: Pero, tú no eres viejo.

Luis: Tengo cuarenta y dos años. Hoy en día eso
significa que soy viejo. Así es la vida.   4.1

4.1 Distinguishing between **ser** and **estar**.

**la merienda está lista   estás temblando   estás de mal humor
no es culpa tuya   tú eres buen trabajador   soy viejo**

● **The problem of ser and estar**

Ser and **estar** both mean **to be**. This can obviously lead to some
confusion, and it is therefore important that you understand the basic
differences between the two verbs. The guidelines given below will
help you to distinguish between the main uses of the two verbs.

Before studying the guidelines however, it is equally important to
realise that **ser** and **estar** do not always fit into neat categories. For
example, one way of distinguishing between the two verbs is to
associate **ser** with the idea of permanence and **estar** with a
temporary state or condition. This distinction is valid up to a point,

but it is contradicted by such examples as **soy rico/soy pobre** (which are not necessarily permanent states) or **está muerto** (which is definitely a permanent condition!).

To complicate matters further, **rico** usually goes with **estar** when it means delicious/tasty (food): *¡Qué rica está la sopa!*

Indeed, quite often it is the context which will determine which verb is to be used. Look at the following examples:

Es triste	=	He's sad (*by nature*).
Está triste	=	He's sad (*at the moment*).
Es listo	=	He's clever.
Está listo	=	He is ready.

In short, when you are reading or listening to Spanish, be alert to specific uses of **ser** and **estar** which may not readily fit into a neat formula.

● **The fundamental difference(s) between ser and estar**

To help you understand the broad difference in usage between **ser** and **estar**, it is worth learning some basic questions by heart before looking at the differences in detail.

a) *¿Cómo es Paco?* = What is Paco like? (*his qualities/ character/nature*)
= What does Paco look like? (*physical description*)

¿Cómo está Paco? = How is Paco? (*physical/emotional condition*)

b) *¿De dónde es Paco?* = Where is Paco from? (*origin/nationality*)
¿Dónde está Paco? = Where is Paco? (*position/location*)

c) *¿Quién es Paco?* = Who is Paco? (*identity*)
¿Quién está hablando? = Who is speaking? (*continuous tense*)

● **When to use ser**

In specific terms, **ser** is used:

a) To say who someone is.
Es mi hermano. Soy Juan.

b) To say what something is.
Es un ordenador. Es una linterna.

c) To show possession.
Es mi coche. Este reloj es de mi hermana.

d) To indicate job/profession/rank/status.
Soy abogado. Es azafata.

e) To indicate origin and nationality.
Soy de Portugal. Son ingleses.

f) To describe a person's character/personal qualities/physical features, and whether young or old.
Es muy simpática. Es alta. Es inteligente. Es tonto. Es gordo. Es joven. Es viejo.

g) To describe the physical qualities of something and to say what it is like.
Es azul. Es redondo. Londres es grande. Es un sitio maravilloso.

h) To comment on the quality of something.
Este libro es interesante. Es muy útil. Es una tontería.

i) To form impersonal phrases.
Es posible. Es necesario.

j) To state the time/date.
Son las tres. Hoy es lunes.

k) To indicate where an event takes place.
La fiesta va a ser en la casa de mi madre.

l) To form the passive.
Huyó sin ser visto. (He fled without being seen.)
Las cartas son recogidas por un empleado. (The letters are collected by an employee.)

● **When to use estar**

In specific terms, **estar** is used:

a) To indicate the whereabouts (position/location) of someone or something.
Mis padres están en Alemania. El libro está en el suelo.

b) To indicate transitory moods/emotions/feelings.
Está enfadado. Está contenta. Está de mal humor.

c) To indicate physical condition.
Estoy bien. Estoy cansado. Estoy enfermo.

d) To comment spontaneously on someone's physical features, indicating your surprise, pleasure...etc at some kind of change/contrast.
¡Qué guapa estás hoy!   = How lovely you are (looking) today!

e) To indicate a temporary state of affairs.
Está de vacaciones.   = He/She is on holiday.
Está de pie.   = He/She is standing.

f) To form the continuous tense.
Te estoy escuchando. Está lloviendo.

g) With the past participle, to describe the result of a previous action.
Estoy casado.   = I'm married.
La puerta está abierta.   = The door is open.
Están sentados.   = They are sitting.

Practice (1): Using ser and estar in natural context

Below you will find an extract from the Spanish novel "Zalacaín el aventurero" by Pío Baroja. Complete the gaps in the dialogue with the correct form (present tense) of either **ser** or **estar**.

(The hero of the novel, Martín, is convalescing after being wounded in battle. He is being looked after by an old couple and their daughter, Rosita, who knows nothing of his past.)

Pronto Martín pudo levantarse y, cojeando, andar por la casa. Un día que contaba su vida y sus aventuras, Rosita le preguntó, de pronto:

—¿Y Catalina, quién .... (1)? ¿........ (2) su novia de usted?
—Sí. ¿Cómo lo sabe usted?
—Porque ha hablado usted mucho de ella durante el delirio.
—¡Ah!

—¿Y .... (3) *guapa?*
—¿*Quién?*
—*Su novia.*
—*Sí, creo que sí.*
—¿*Cómo? ¿Cree usted nada más?*
—...... (4) *que la conozco desde chico y* .... (5) *tan acostumbrado a verla, que casi no sé cómo* .... (6).
—*Pero, ¿no* .... (7) *usted enamorado de ella?*
—*No sé, la verdad.*
—¡*Qué cosa más rara! ¿Qué aspecto tiene?*
—........ (8) *algo rubia...*
—¿*Y tiene hermosos ojos?*
—*No tanto como usted* —*dijo Martín.*

A Rosita Briones le centellearon los ojos y envolvió a Martín en una de sus miradas enigmáticas.

Practice (2): Recognising when to use **ser** and **estar**

Complete the gaps below with the correct form (present tense) of **ser** or **estar**.

1 ¿*De quién* .... *este abrigo?*

2 *El señor Ramos no* ....*en la oficina;* .... *en casa.*

3 *Moscú* .... *la capital de Rusia.*

4 *El Everest* .... *la montaña más alta del mundo.*

5 ¿*Quién* .... *gritando?*

6 *Mi madre* .... *enfermera.*

7 *Mi madre* .... *enferma.*

8 *Esta camisa* .... *rota.*

9 .... *la una de la tarde.*

10 *La tienda* .... *cerrada.*

11 *Ella* .... *morena, alta y delgada.*

12 ¡*Qué morena* .... *tú! ¿Qué has hecho para ponerte tan morena?*

13 ¿*De dónde* .... *Fernando?*

14 ¿*Dónde* .... *los servicios?*

15 ¿*Dónde* .... *la fiesta, en tu piso o en la casa de Pedro?*

16 *La agencia de viajes .... cerca de la estación.*

17 *Mi tío .... muy distraído. Se olvida de todo.*

18 *—¿Cuál .... tu profesión?*

—........médico.

19 *—¿Cómo .... tu madre?*

—........mucho mejor, gracias.

20 *—¿Cómo .... Antonio?*

—...... rubio y muy guapo.

21 *—¿Cuánto .... en total?*

—........ quinientas pesetas.

22 *—¿Desde hace cuánto tiempo .... usted aquí en Barcelona?*

—........ en Barcelona desde hace tres meses.

23 *Los ingleses tienen fama de .... muy fríos.*

24 *¡La sopa .... fría!*

25 *Yo .... harto de tus mentiras. ¿Por qué no me dices la verdad?*

26 *Hola, María. ¡Qué bonita ....hoy!*

27 *—¿........ usted casado?*

—No, ...soltero.

28 *¿........solo, o tienes compañía?*

29 *Vosotros .... estudiantes, ¿verdad?*

30 *¿Queréis seguir, o ya .... cansados?*

Extra reference

✦ When not to use **un/una** after **ser**

The indefinite article **un/una** is not used after **ser** when describing someone's religious or political persuasion, job, rank or status.

Soy protestante, pero mi esposa es católica. = I am a protestant, but my wife is a catholic.

Mi hermano es socialista. = My brother is a socialist.

Mi sobrino es escritor. = My nephew is an author.

Mi sobrina es profesora. = My niece is a teacher.

However, the indefinite article is used if the noun is qualified by an adjective.

Mi sobrino es un escritor famoso. = My nephew is a famous author.

Michael Caine es un gran actor. = Michael Caine is a great actor.

Ella es una gran cantante y actriz. = She is a great singer and actress.

(Note that **grande** becomes **gran** when placed in front of a noun, and that the meaning changes from **big** to **great**.)

✦ Developing vocabulary

Note carefully the following phrases used with **estar**:

a) *Estar acostumbrado a hacer algo* = To be used to doing something.

b) *Estar a punto de hacer algo* = To be about to do something/to be on the point of doing something.

You may also come across **estar para** in certain fixed phrases:

El tren está para salir. = The train is about to/ready to leave.

c) *Está bien.* = That's fine. / Agreed. / O.K.

4.2 Distinguishing between ¿Qué? and ¿Cuál?.

¿Cuál es el problema?   ¿Qué ha sucedido?
¿Qué es lo que pasa?   ¿Qué noticia?

● The problem of translating **which?** and **what?** into Spanish

¿Cuál? can mean **which?** or **what?**
¿Qué? can mean **which?** or **what?**

These two simple words can cause a great deal of confusion, so study very carefully the following points:

● **1) Which?**

If you wish to make a distinction between two items or more, you can use either **¿qué?** or **¿cuál?**. The difference between the two words is as follows:

a) **¿Qué?** goes directly with the noun it is referring to.

¿De qué andén sale el tren? = From which platform does the train leave?

¿Qué libro quieres? = Which book do you want?

¿Qué camisa te gusta más? = Which shirt do you prefer?

b) **¿Cuál?** never goes directly with the noun it is referring to (except in very colloquial speech).

¿Cuál de estas camisas te gusta más? = Which of these shirts do you prefer?

¿Cuál te gusta más? = Which one do you prefer?

¿Cuál prefieres, la blanca o la azul? = Which (one) do you prefer, the white one or the blue one?

¿Cuál es mi habitación? = Which is my room?

● **2) What?**

Generally speaking, **what...?** is translated by **¿qué...?**:

¿Qué? ¿qué? ¿qué dices?

¿Qué quieres? = What do you want?

¿Qué tienes? = What have you got?

However, a problem arises when we wish to translate **what is...?**.

a) **What is…?** becomes **¿qué es…?** when you are being asked to <u>define</u> something.

¿Qué es esto?   = What is this?

¿Qué es un 'duro'?   = What is a 'duro'?

Your answer will be a <u>definition</u> of some kind:

Es un libro.   = It is a book.

Es una moneda de cinco pesetas. = It is a five-peseta coin.

b) **What is…?** becomes **¿cuál es…?** when the person wants to know a particular detail (or specific details).

¿Cuál es el problema?   = What is the problem? (*Tell me about it.*)

¿Cuál es tu plato preferido?   = What is your favourite dish?

¿Cuál es la capital de España? = What is the capital of Spain?

¿Cuáles son tus pasatiempos? = What are your hobbies?

In this type of question, you are being asked to specify something within a defined area. The person is seeking further information/ description ("I know you have got a problem. I want to know what it is." or "I know that Spain has a capital city. I want to know what it is."). Your options are more limited when considering an answer to this type of question, whereas your options are open when considering a **¿qué es…?** type of question.

Practice (3): Recognising when to use ¿qué? and ¿cuál?

Complete each gap below with **qué** or **cuál/cuáles**.

1 ¿........ *deportes practicas?*

2 ¿........ *número gastas?*

3 ¿........ *es tu número de teléfono?*

4 ¿........ *es el prefijo de Santander?*

5 ¿........ *asignatura te gusta menos?*

6 ¿........ *es tu asignatura preferida?*

7 ¿........ *es tu padre?*

8 ¿........ *es su ocupación?*

9 ¿........ *es 'karoake'?*

10 ¿........ *son tus aficiones?*

11 ¿*En* .... *piso vives?*

12 ¿........ *clase de ropa tiene?*

13 ¿........ *prefieres, el rojo o el blanco?*

14 ¿........ *es la mejor revista de modas?*

15 ¿........ *es tu opinión?*

16 ¿........ *es su motivo?*

17 ¿........ *es la diferencia entre esta máquina y ésa?*

18 ¿........ *periódico has comprado?*

Extra reference

✦ **¿Qué es lo que...?** = What...?

Note how one can make a general question more specific and emphatic by adding **es lo que** to **¿Qué?**:

¿Qué buscas? = What are you looking for?

¿Qué es lo que buscas? = What actually are you looking for?/ What is it that you are looking for?

4.3 Forming and using the Present Continuous tense.

estás temblando   ¿por qué estás llorando?
no estamos peleando   estás gritando

● **The formation of the Present Continuous**

Such phrases as **estás temblando** (you are trembling) and **estás gritando** (you are shouting) are examples of the Present Continuous tense. This tense is formed by the present tense of **estar** + the Present Participle (or *gerundio*) of the main verb.

The Present Participle (or *gerundio*) is formed in the following way:

a) -AR verbs: Remove the -**ar** from the infinitive and add -**ando**.

cocinar (to cook):   *cocinando* (cooking)

dar (to give):   *dando* (giving)

b) -ER and -IR verbs: Remove the -**er** or -**ir** from the infinitive and add -**iendo**.

beber (to drink):   *bebiendo* (drinking)

vivir (to live):   *viviendo* (living)

c) Spelling changes.

For reasons of pronunciation, -**iendo** usually becomes -**yendo** when placed next to a vowel.

caer: cayendo (falling); *creer: creyendo* (believing); *construir: construyendo* (building); *leer: leyendo* (reading); *oír: oyendo* (hearing); *traer: trayendo* (bringing).

(This rule does not apply to *seguir/conseguir*.)

d) Radical-changing -IR verbs.

When you remove the -**ir** from the infinitive, you are left with what we call the stem of the verb. A change is required in the stem: **e** becomes **i** and **o** becomes **u**.

sentir: sintiendo (feeling); *pedir: pidiendo* (asking for); *reír: riendo* (laughing); *dormir: durmiendo* (sleeping); *seguir: siguiendo* (following).

e) There are a few irregular present participles that need to be learnt by heart:

decir: diciendo (saying); *ir: yendo* (going); *poder: pudiendo* (being able to).

● **Using the Present Continuous.**

a) Both in English and in Spanish, this tense makes clear that something is happening/in progress at a particular moment. This tense is also used, both in English and in Spanish, to show that an action is temporary.

Están jugando.   = They are playing.

¿Qué estás comiendo? = What are you eating?

Está nevando.   = It is snowing.

b) In English the Present Continuous can denote the future, but this is not the case in Spanish. When referring to the future, do not put such verbs as *ir, venir, llegar* and *volver* into the Present Continuous.

They are going to Madrid next week. = Van a Madrid la semana que viene.

They are coming tomorrow. = Vienen/Van a venir mañana.

She is arriving this afternoon. = Llega/Va a llegar esta tarde.

I am not coming/going back. = No vuelvo/No voy a volver.

c) In English we use the present participle to describe position and posture (*sitting, standing, lying, leaning*), whereas in Spanish the past participle (or a suitable phrase) is used instead. This is because in English we focus on the activity itself, whereas in Spanish the emphasis is on the present state being the result of a previous action.

She is sitting. = *Está sentada.*

They are standing. = *Están de pie.*

There's Fernando, leaning against the wall.
Allí está Fernando, apoyado en la pared.

There is a man leaning out of the window.
Hay un hombre asomado a la ventana.

Here I am, lying on the beach,...
Aquí estoy, tumbado en la playa,...

There's someone lying on the floor; I think he's dead.
Hay alguien tendido en el suelo; parece que está muerto.

NB: The past participle acts like an adjective when used with **estar** or on its own.

Está sentado/a. Están sentados/as.

The Present Participle, however, never changes its form and so will always end in **-o**.

Estoy corriendo. Estamos corriendo. Están corriendo.

Practice (4): Using the present continuous

Using the clues given underneath, fill in the missing words (they are all
present participles) in the grid below. The completed grid will reveal
another present participle. What is the word? Number 2 has been done
for you as an example.

```
1   __ __|__|__ __ __ __ __
2    T  O |M |A  N  D  O
3   __ __|__|__ __ __ __ __
4   __ __|__|__ __ __ __ __
5      __|__|__ __ __ __ __ __ __ __
6   __ __|__|__ __ __ __ __
7 __ __ __|__|__ __ __ __ __
8   __ __|__|__ __ __ __
9      __|__|__ __ __ __ __ __ __ __ __
10  __ __|__|__ __ __ __ __ __ __ __
11  __ __|__|__ __ __ __ __
12  __ __|__|__ __ __ __ __
```

1   *Me estás .... mentiras. Dime la verdad.*

2   *¿Me estás .... el pelo?*

3   *Te estás .... muy gordo. Tienes que seguir un régimen.*

4   *Estoy .... trabajo. Llevo seis meses sin trabajar.*

5   *Estás .... demasiado. Tienes que tomar unas vacaciones.*

6   *No hagas ruido. Papá está acostado. Está ....*

7   *¡Tú no estás .... mis instrucciones! Así no se hace.*

8   *—¿Qué estás .... ? —Una novela policíaca.*

9   *Estoy .... una carta a mi madre.*

10   *Estás .... demasiado rápido. Vamos a tener un accidente.*

11   *¿Qué hacen esos mendigos? ¿Están .... dinero?*

12   *Mira, está .... ¿Tienes un paraguas?*

Practice (5): Recognising translation problems with the present continuous

Translate the following into Spanish:

1 Who is the girl sitting at the table?

2 They are arriving tomorrow at ten o'clock.

3 They are chatting in the kitchen.

4 Why is the dog barking? (use *ladrar*)

5 Can you see Pedro? He is leaning out of the window.

6 You are coughing a lot. Are you all right? (use *toser*)

7 That boy leaning against the wall is Andrea's boyfriend.

8 I am going to France tomorrow and I am not coming back until next week.

9 She's lying on the floor, doing exercises. (use *tumbar*)

10 Why are you standing? Why don't you sit down?

Extra reference

✦ Further translation problems associated with the Present Participle

There are various problems involved in translating the ...**ing** form (Present Participle) from English into Spanish. We have already seen, for example, the problem of translating such words as **sitting** and **leaning**. Note also the following points:

a) In English the ...**ing** form of the verb automatically follows a preposition (in, on, with, after, before, for...etc). In Spanish the infinitive automatically follows a preposition.

After drinking the coffee, he...	= *Después de tomar el café, él...*
Before starting, we...	= *Antes de empezar, nosotros...*
On arriving home, they...	= *Al llegar a casa, ellos...*
...without thinking.	= *...sin pensar.*

b) In English we often use 'by + ...ing' to say how something is done. In Spanish there is no need to translate 'by'.

—¿*Cómo lo abriste?*	= How did you open it?
—*Apretando este botón.*	= By pressing this button.

4.4 Using Object Pronouns with the Present Continuous

algo te está fastidiando   no te estoy gritando

● Listing the three types of object pronoun

There are three basic types of personal object pronoun: direct (eg I saw <u>him</u>), indirect (eg He spoke <u>to her</u>), and reflexive (eg She is fooling <u>herself</u>).
In Spanish these pronouns are grouped as follows:

(Subject)	Direct Object	Indirect Object	Reflexive
(yo)	*me*	*me*	*me*
(tú)	*te*	*te*	*te*
(él/ella/Vd)	*lo/le, la*	*le*	*se*
(nosotros/as)	*nos*	*nos*	*nos*
(vosotros/as)	*os*	*os*	*os*
(ellos/as, Vds)	*los/les, las*	*les*	*se*

● Understanding where and when problems may arise when using object pronouns

i) We can see from the lists above that **me, te, nos** and **os** pose no problems in usage because they function as direct, indirect and reflexive pronouns.

ii) We can also see that **se** is the reflexive pronoun for the third person (singular and plural).

iii) It is also clear from the lists that **le**, as an indirect object pronoun, can be translated as 'to him/to her/to it/to you'; and that **les** can be translated as 'to them/to you'. To avoid possible confusion, **le** may be accompanied by **a él, a ella** or **a usted**. Likewise, **les** may be accompanied by **a ellos, a ellas** or **a ustedes**.

Le interesa a ella.   = It interests her. / It is of interest to her.

Les digo a ustedes.   = I tell you. / I say to you.

iv) It is only with the third person direct object pronouns that there are some problems of usage.

Technically, only **lo** should be used for 'him', 'you' or 'it' (masculine/neutral); just as **la** is used for 'her', 'you' or 'it' (feminine). With **la** usage is clear, but not so with **lo**. Many educated Spanish people prefer to use **lo** just for 'it', and **le** for 'him' or 'you'. This is very sensible and logical.

The same problem arises, but to a lesser extent, with the plural form. Technically, **los** should be used for people and things. In practice, however, **les** is often used for people.

Basically, it is up to you to select the usage that you are happiest with. Perhaps the most sensible approach – and one adopted by many modern writers – is to use **lo** for 'it' and **le** for 'him/you', but to use **los** for 'them' whenever it is grammatically clear that a direct object pronoun is required. If in doubt, use **les**.

- Positioning an object pronoun with the present continuous

When used with the Present Continuous, an object pronoun may be placed either in front of **estar** or added to the Present Participle (in which case an accent is required).

Estoy limpiando la alfombra.	= I am cleaning the carpet.
(Yo) la estoy limpiando.	= I am cleaning it.
Estoy limpiándola.	= I am cleaning it.

- The rules of stress and accentuation

In order to fully understand why and when an accent needs to be placed on a word, it is necessary to learn the basic rules regarding stress and accentuation. These rules are very straightforward and well worth learning by heart.

i) Stress in pronunciation:

If a word ends in a **vowel**, or in **n** or **s**, the penultimate (the last but one) syllable is stressed.

contento; inglesa; crimen; ingleses; estaciones.

If the word ends in a consonant other than **n** or **s**, the last syllable is stressed.

azul; cenar; ciudad; feliz.

ii) Adding an accent:

If the word is to be stressed in some way contrary to the two rules outlined above, then an accent (´) is placed over that syllable.

débil; chófer; jardín; jóvenes; inglés; estación.

When adding anything extra to a word, the rule is that the original stress of that word should be retained. That is why an accent is required when an object pronoun is added to a present participle.

—*¿Estás haciendo tus deberes?*

—*Sí, los estoy haciendo.*

—*Sí, estoy haciéndolos.*

NB: On the other hand, we do not need an extra accent when we add an object pronoun to an infinitive because the original stress does not change.

—*¿Vas a hacer tus deberes?*

—*Sí, los voy a hacer ahora mismo.*

—*Sí, voy a hacerlos ahora mismo.*

(Note that, just as with the present continuous, we can choose where to place an object pronoun with an infinitive construction: either in front of the first verb or added to the infinitive.)

Practice (6): Recognising where and when to place an accent with verbs

Rewrite the following sentences. In each case, add the object pronoun to the present participle or the infinitive.

1 *Lo estamos haciendo.*

2 *Lo están revisando.*

3 *Los estoy contando.*

4 *Lo quiero terminar cuanto antes.*

5 *¿Lo estás copiando?*

6 *Le estamos escuchando.*

7 *Las están cambiando.*

8 *Nos están esperando.*

9 *Te voy a decir una cosa.*

10 *La estamos examinando.*

11 *Lo estoy leyendo.*

12 *Se está lavando las manos.*

13 *Me voy a lavar las manos.*

14 *Los niños se están bañando en el río.*

15 *No lo estamos tocando.*

16 *No nos están mirando.*

17 *Nos tienen que pagar.*

18 *¡Lo están rompiendo!*

19 *Lo vamos a pintar.*

20 *Lo estoy reparando.*

Extra reference

✦ Understanding the various functions of the indirect object pronoun

A common mistake is to think of the indirect object pronoun as only meaning 'to me, to you, to him...'. The more you read and listen to Spanish, the more aware you will become of the fact that the indirect object pronoun has a variety of functions. Here are some examples:

i) The indirect object pronoun is often used as an ornament when a person is the object of a verb. This usage is obligatory if two objects (a thing and a person) follow a verb, but optional (and generally omitted) if just a person is the object of a verb. (See also 10.4)

Voy a darle un regalo a Antonio. = I am going to give Antonio a present.

Voy a visitar a María. = I am going to visit María.

ii) It is used with verbs of removal, in place of a possessive word like 'my', 'his', or 'their'.

Quieren quitarle el bebé a ella. = They want to take away her baby.

Quieren robarme el dinero. = They want to steal my money.

Notice that in the examples above the pronoun has the idea of *from*.

iii) It can mean **for**...

Te tengo un regalo. = I've got a present for you.

(or you can say: Tengo un regalo para ti.)

iv) It is used with **tener** when emotions are being expressed.

Les tiene miedo. = He's afraid of them.

Les tiene odio.   = He loathes them.

v) Just as the reflexive form is used for **self** when parts of the body/items of clothing are the object of a verb, so too the indirect object pronoun is used when somebody else's personal possessions are affected by an active verb.

Voy a besarle la mano. = I am going to kiss her/his hand.

Te voy a cortar el pelo. = I am going to cut your hair.

Después de estrecharle la mano, yo... = After shaking his/her hand, I...

4.5 Forming and using the Present Perfect tense.

¿qué ha sucedido? ¿he hecho yo algo? te he dicho   he recibido ¿qué ha ocurrido? me han despedido ha perdido

● **What is the Present Perfect tense?**

Such phrases as *¿qué ha sucedido?* (What has happened?), *te he dicho* (I have told you) and *he recibido* (I have received) are examples of the Present Perfect tense.

● **Forming the Present Perfect tense**

This tense is formed by the present tense of **haber (he, has, ha, hemos, habéis, han)** + the Past Participle.

The Past Participle is formed in the following way:

i) -AR verbs: Remove the **-ar** from the infinitive and add **-ado**.

dar (to give):   *dado* (given)

hablar (to speak): *hablado* (spoken)

ii) -ER and -IR verbs: Remove the **-er/-ir** from the infinitive and add **-ido**.

comer (to eat):   *comido* (eaten)
sentir (to feel):   *sentido* (felt)
ir (to go):   *ido* (gone)

iii) An accent is required when **-ido** is placed next to a vowel:

caer caído (fallen); *creer creído* (believed); *oír oído* (heard); *leer leído* (read); *traer traído* (brought).

This rule does not apply to verbs ending in **-uir**:

construir construido (built); *huir huido* (fled); *seguir seguido* (followed).

iv) The following irregular past participles should be learnt by heart:

abrir abierto (opened); *cubrir cubierto* (covered); *decir dicho* (said); *escribir escrito* (written); *freír frito* (fried); *hacer hecho* (done/made); *morir muerto* (died/dead); *poner puesto* (put); *romper roto* (broken); *ver visto* (seen); *volver vuelto* (returned).

v) When used with **haber** to form the Present Perfect tense, the Past Participle never changes its form and so will always end in **-o**.

● **Using the Present Perfect tense**

Look carefully at the following examples of the Present Perfect. Note the word order in each case. You will notice that **haber** and the Past Participle are never separated/split up when forming the Present Perfect tense.

i) Statement
    Ella ha cambiado mucho.   = She has changed a lot.
    Ha dejado de llover.   = It has stopped raining.

ii) Negative statement
    No he visto esa película.   = I haven't seen that film.
    Nunca he viajado en avión.   = I have never travelled by plane.
    No han aprendido nada.   = They have learnt nothing.

iii) Question
    ¿Ha llegado el correo?   = Has the post arrived?
    ¿Ha empezado el programa?   = Has the programme started?

iv) With an object pronoun

Lo he visto.	=	I have seen it.
No lo he tocado.	=	I haven't touched it.
Me he cortado el dedo.	=	I have cut my finger.
Usted se ha equivocado.	=	You have made a mistake. / You are mistaken.
¿Se ha levantado Pedro?	=	Has Pedro got up?

● You should have no difficulty in deciding when to use the Present Perfect because – apart from the time constructions which you studied in Unit 3 – English and Spanish usage is almost identical.

Practice (7): Constructing phrases with the Present Perfect tense

Rewrite the following sentences, placing the words in their correct order.

1 *en han matemáticas suspendido me.*
2 *bien ella muy portado se ha.*
3 *escrito han me no.*
4 *a montado he nunca caballo.*
5 *¡quemado me he!*
6 *¿pasado has lo tal qué?*
7 *hemos lo bien muy pasado.*
8 *he me mucho divertido.*
9 *tobillo me el he torcido.*
10 *¿comprado Ana ha qué?*

Practice (8): Using the Present Perfect tense in context

Change each verb in brackets into the correct form of the Present Perfect.

a) —*¿Por qué (parar) el tren?*
—*(Haber) un accidente.*
—*¿Qué (ocurrir)?*
—*No sé. Voy a averiguar.*

b) —*Tu madre me (decir) que tú (decidirse) a dejar tu trabajo. ¿Es cierto?*
—*Sí, es verdad. Yo (dimitir).*
—*Pero, ¿por qué?*

—*Unos amigos míos (poner) una agencia de viajes y están buscando otro socio. Yo siempre (querer) trabajar por mi cuenta y, como (ahorrar) bastante dinero en los últimos cinco años, tengo suficiente capital para juntarme con ellos.*

c) —*¿Dónde está Felipe? ¿(Irse) a algún sitio?*
—*No, (acostarse).*
—*¿Tan temprano?*
—*Sí, hoy le (tocar) trabajar muy duro. Está deshecho.*

d) —*(Leer) esta novela?*
—*Sí, dos veces. Me encanta. Esta novela me (enseñar) muchas cosas. Me (abrir) los ojos. Te digo sinceramente que esta novela me (hacer) apreciar las cosas en su justo valor.*
—*La escribió mi abuela.*
—*¡No me digas!*

e) —*¿(Hacer) tus deberes?*
—*Sí, mamá.*
—*¿(Arreglar) tu cuarto?*
—*Sí, mamá.*
—*¿(Dar) de comer a los conejitos?*
—*Sí, mamá.*
—*¿(Lavarse) las manos?*
—*Sí, mamá.*
—*¿(Poner) la mesa?*
—*Sí, mamá.*
—*Entonces sí puedes ver la televisión.*
—*Gracias, mamá.*

Extra reference

✦ **Difference in English and Spanish usage of the Present Perfect**

There is one use of the Present Perfect in Spanish that does not correspond to its usage in English. If an event is very recent (it happened just now; or it is very fresh in the memory because it occurred in the previous six hours or so), the Present Perfect may be used in preference to the Preterite (past simple).

¿Quién ha sido? = Who was it? (I want to know who did that/said that just now.)

✦ **Avoiding the passive when using the present perfect**

Where possible, the passive is usually avoided in Spanish – especially with the Present and Present Perfect. One easy – and very natural – way of avoiding the passive is to make 'they' the subject of the verb in question.

Me han despedido. = I have been sacked. (They have sacked me.)

Me han robado. = I have been robbed. (They have robbed me.)

Me han aceptado. = I have been accepted. (They have accepted me.)

✦ **Recognising the Present Perfect Continuous tense**

The Present Perfect Continuous tense is formed in the following way:

Haber + **estado** + present participle

Ha estado trabajando toda la noche.
He has been working all night.

He estado mirando las fotos de nuestra boda.
I've been looking at our wedding photos.

Ha estado bebiendo mucho últimamente.
He has been drinking a lot recently.

4.6 Levantar + object   *(reference only)*

¿Es que no puedo levantar la voz de vez en cuando?

We saw in Unit 2 that most active verbs usually need a reflexive pronoun when used with parts of the body or clothing. There are, however, exceptions to the rule. **Levantar** (to raise) and **bajar** (to lower) do not become reflexive when followed by an object noun, but we still need to apply the rule that parts of the body are usually described in an impersonal way (with **el/la/los/las**). You should also note that, in literary Spanish, **alzar** is often used instead of **levantar**.

Look carefully at the following examples:

Levantando los brazos al cielo, lanzó un grito horrible.
Raising his arms to the sky, he let out a horrible cry.

Levantó los ojos/la mirada/la vista y la vio delante de él.
He looked up and saw her in front of him.

Dándose cuenta de que todos la escuchaban, ella bajó la voz.
Realising that everybody was listening to her, she lowered her voice.

NB: You should also note that **abrir, cerrar** and **volver** follow the same pattern as **levantar** and **bajar**.

Abre la boca.   = Open your mouth.

Cierra los ojos.   = Close your eyes.

Volvió la espalda.   = He turned his back.

Progress test 4

Translate the following into Spanish.

1 What's Camilo like?
2 Where is Nuria from?
3 How are your parents?
4 My mother is an actress. In my opinion, she is a great actress.
5 Is she married or is she single?
6 What's the problem? Why are you in a bad mood?
7 What are you reading? Is it interesting?
8 He's not listening to us. Is he sleeping?
9 They are getting up.
10 They have got up.
11 I've been robbed!
12 He's been sacked.
13 Has Pedro come back?
14 We haven't seen her.
15 I've been cheated! (use *engañar*)

UNIT 5 Contrasting the past with the present

Carlos, a student, and his grandfather are discussing the changes that have occurred in Spain since 1975 – when Franco died and Spain, after many years of dictatorship, became a democratic country.

Carlos: A pesar de <u>todos los problemas sociales y</u> <u>económicos que España</u> tiene hoy en día, por lo menos podemos actuar con más libertad que antes. 5.3/5.4

Abuelo: Y, ¿de qué nos sirve esta libertad? Además, te digo una cosa, <u>no es la libertad sino el libertinaje</u> lo que 5.6 tenemos aquí en España. <u>La democracia</u> nos ha 5.2 traído muy pocas ventajas. <u>Lo que sí veo</u> por todas 5.4 partes es la pornografía, la violencia, la droga, la corrupción, el desempleo y la inseguridad.

Carlos: Por lo menos vivimos en una sociedad moderna, no como antes.

Abuelo: <u>Antes se vivía mejor.</u> Los jóvenes y los viejos <u>se</u> 5.1 <u>respetaban</u> mutuamente. <u>Si no te metías en</u> 5.1 política, <u>nadie te molestaba.</u> Antes, por ejemplo, <u>tú</u> 5.1 <u>podías dar un paseo</u> a cualquier hora sin miedo de 5.7 ser atacado por gamberros o drogadictos.

Carlos: Tenemos nuestros problemas sociales, de acuerdo, pero los cambios políticos han sido muy positivos.   5.6

Abuelo: ¿Tú crees? En primer lugar, a mí no me interesa la   5.2
política. Los políticos son todos iguales. Son unos   5.2
mentirosos y sólo les interesa el poder. Además, los
jóvenes de hoy no aprecian la libertad. No respetan   5.2
la ley. Rechazan la disciplina, la familia... Yo no   5.2
sé. Lo que es verdaderamente triste es que los   5.4
jóvenes de hoy no tenéis escrúpulos.

Carlos: ¡Hombre, abuelito, estás exagerando un poco! ¿no?

Abuelo: No creo. Un ejemplo claro es el aborto. No lo   5.1
teníamos anteriormente. El respeto a la vida   5.2
significa el no matar a un indefenso. Llegando al
extremo de matar a un indefenso es el punto
culminante de ya no tener escrúpulos, ¿no?

Carlos: Bueno, en eso quizá te doy la razón, no sé. Es   5.7
un tema bastante complicado. Sin embargo ha   5.3
habido cambios positivos, ¿no crees?

Abuelo: Pues sí, claro que sí; pero al fin y al cabo España
en mi opinión ha perdido más de lo que ha ganado   5.5
en los últimos veinte años.

Carlos: No estoy de acuerdo.

(Entra la abuela.)

Abuela: Bueno, familia, yo quería echarme una siesta, pero   5.1
con tanto ruido no puedo. Tú, Carlos, amor de mi
vida, en vez de perder el tiempo discutiendo con tu
abuelo, ¿por qué no sacas al perro? Anda, el perro
te está esperando en el pasillo. Y, ¿quién ha estado
fumando? Julio, mi amor, tú sabes muy bien que
el médico te ha prohibido fumar.

Abuelo: *(con una sonrisa filosófica):* Ciertas cosas no han
cambiado en esta casa y nunca van a cambiar.
¡Vamos, Carlos, al parque con el perro! Yo te
acompaño. Hasta luego, querida.

5.1 Recognising and using the Imperfect Tense.

**antes se vivía mejor   se respetaban   sí no te metías en
nadie te molestaba   tú podías
no lo teníamos anteriormente   yo quería**

● Forming the Imperfect tense

The Imperfect tense is formed in the following way:

a) -AR verbs: Remove the **-ar** from the infinitive and add **-aba,
-abas, -aba, -ábamos, -abais, -aban.**

*hablar: hablaba, hablabas, hablaba, hablábamos,
hablabais, hablaban.*

b) -ER and -IR verbs: Remove the **-er/-ir** from the infinitive and add
-ía, -ías, -ía, -íamos, -íais, -ían.

comer: comía, comías, comía, comíamos, comíais, comían.

vivir: vivía, vivías, vivía, vivíamos, vivíais, vivían.

c) There are only three exceptions to the above:

Ser	Ir	Ver
era	*iba*	*veía*
eras	*ibas*	*veías*
era	*iba*	*veía*
éramos	*íbamos*	*veíamos*
erais	*ibais*	*veíais*
eran	*iban*	*veían*

● Using the Imperfect tense

The Imperfect tense is used in the following ways:

a) It can be used as an alternative to the Imperfect Continuous tense
(**estaba haciendo**). In other words, you can always use the
Imperfect tense instead of the Imperfect Continuous.

Yo estaba diciendo que ... = I was saying that...
   (Imperfect Continuous)
Yo decía que...   = I was saying that... (Imperfect)

b) It is used to describe past habitual action. This may cause some problems when translating because in English past habitual action is rendered by **the past simple/used to/would**. Look carefully at the following examples:

We always ate fish on Friday(s).
Siempre comíamos pescado los viernes.

I used to see her every day. = *Yo la veía todos los días.*

He would always smoke a cigar after lunch.
Siempre fumaba un puro después del almuerzo.

c) Just as in English we use **used to** or **would to** reinforce the idea of a past habitual action, so too in Spanish the Imperfect of **soler** + infinitive can be used to emphasise a past habit.

Solíamos ir a Francia todos los años.
We used to go to France every year.

Solía beber mucho. = He used to drink a lot.

d) The Imperfect tense is used for open-ended description in the past (when the time framework is very general). It is also used to establish the background to an event/story.

Cuando yo tenía diez años, quería ser cura.
When I was ten, I wanted to be a priest.

Una vez, hace muchísimos años, vivía en Segovia un carpintero que se llamaba Pedro Sánchez. Era viudo y tenía diez hijos.
Once, many years ago, there lived in Segovia a carpenter called Pedro Sánchez. He was a widower and had ten children.

e) Just as the Present tense is used instead of the Present Perfect in specific time constructions, so too the Imperfect is used instead of the Past Perfect (or Pluperfect) in such constructions.

Acababa de llegar. = He had just arrived.

Llevaba diez años trabajando allí.
He had been working there for ten years.

Era médico desde hacía cuatro años.
He had been a doctor for four years.

Practice (1): Using the Imperfect tense in context (past description and habitual action)

In the following three passages, change each verb in brackets into the correct form of the Imperfect tense.

a) *Érase una vez un rey llamado Midas que (vivir) en un palacio resplandeciente y (tener) casi todo lo que un ser humano (poder) desear: una buena esposa, una bella hija rubia, un gato de ojos verdes, platos de oro, plata y un palacio lleno de criados que le (servir) a él y a su familia.*

Pero Midas (estar) malhumorado. Su único placer (ser) atesorar oro, y nunca (parecer) tener bastante. (Amar) tanto el oro que incluso a su hija la (llamar) María Oro. (Pasar) muchas horas al día contando las monedas. Y antes de irse a la cama (abrir) los cofres en que las (guardar) para mirarlas y tocarlas.

Un día que (estar) acariciando su oro, una sombra temblorosa se le apareció......

b) *El elefante del parque zoológico (acabar) de morir, y el guardián (llorar) amargamente.*

—¡Vamos, vamos! dijo una señora que (pasar) por allí. —¡Tenga valor, hombre! Ya me imagino que usted (querer) mucho al pobre animal después de cuidarlo tantos años.

—¡Qué va! No tiene nada que ver, exclamó el guardián en tono desesperado.

—El problema es que a mí me toca enterrarlo.

c) *Hace tiempo, el apretón de manos (ser) una forma de decir: "Puedes fiarte de mí".*

Un hombre (tender) la mano a otro para demostrarle que no (ir) a desenvainar la espada. Si el otro le (tender) a su vez la mano, (unirse) las dos en un fuerte apretón. Así (ver) cada uno que el otro no (empuñar) ningún arma y (saber) que (poder) fiarse de él.

Hoy no ceñimos espada; sin embargo, el apretón de manos puede significar todavía: "confía en mí".

Practice (2): Contrasting past habitual action with the present

Change each verb in brackets into either the correct form of the Imperfect tense or the Present tense.

1 *Cuando (ser) novios, nosotros (salir) todos los fines de semana; pero ahora que (estar) casados, nunca (salir).*

2 *Yo (leer) mucho cuando (ser) más joven, pero ya no (leer) tanto.*

3 *Antes mi padre (fumar) treinta cigarrillos al día, pero ahora (fumar) menos de diez a la semana.*

4 *Yo (soler) visitar a mi tía muy a menudo cuando ella (vivir) en la misma calle que nosotros; pero ahora ella (vivir) en otra ciudad y sólo (verse) cada cuatro o cinco meses.*

5 *Hace miles de años, los hombres (creer) que el dios llamado Zeus (proteger) el cielo y la tierra. Una vez cada cuatro años, los habitantes de Olimpia (celebrar) una fiesta en honor de Zeus. Hoy, más de dos mil años después, atletas de todo el mundo (reunirse) cada cuatro años para celebrar los Juegos Olímpicos.*

Extra reference

The Imperfect form of **hay** (there is/are) is **había** (there was/were).

Había una vez un chico que…	= There was once a boy who…
Había muchos niños esperando…	= There were many children waiting…

5.2 Talking about people or things in general.

La democracia   no me interesa la política   Los políticos son
no aprecian la libertad   rechazan la disciplina
el respeto a la vida

- **The difference between English and Spanish when referring to things in general**

    In English when we refer to an idea in general or to things or people in general, we do not use 'the' with a noun.
    eg Life is not easy.   I don't like beer.   Nurses do not earn a lot of money.

    In Spanish, however, when a noun is used in a general sense it usually has to have the definite article (**el/la/los/las**).

    La vida no es fácil.

    No me gusta la cerveza.

    Las enfermeras no ganan mucho dinero.

Practice (3): Making general statements

Match items 1–15 with items a–o.

  1 *La pereza es*
  2 *El amor es*
  3 *Las serpientes*
  4 *No me gustan*
  5 *Me gusta*
  6 *La vida es*
  7 *La contaminación es*
  8 *Los coches son útiles, pero*
  9 *Los artistas*
10 *La mejor receta para combatir la sed*
11 *Los libros viejos son*
12 *¡Así es*
13 *Los parques zoológicos son unos lugares*
14 *Los insecticidas no sólo matan a los insectos*
15 *Se dice que el dinero es el origen*

a *es el agua templada con limón.*
b *no tienen patas.*
c *madre de la pobreza.*
d *ciego.*
e *un problema mundial.*
f *nacen, no se hacen.*
g *la natación.*
h *dura.*
i *contaminan el ambiente.*
j *los perros.*
k *de todos nuestros males.*
l *sino también a otros animales.*
m *la vida!*
n *como los viejos amigos.*
o *en los cuales los animales están enjaulados para que la gente los pueda ver.*

Extra reference

✦ When to retain and when to drop the definite article

In Spanish when a noun of a general nature is the subject of a verb it will always take the definite article (**el/la/los/las**).

El café no es bueno para la salud.
Coffee is not good for your health.

However, matters are not so clear cut when the noun is the object of a verb or when it follows a preposition. Study carefully the following points:

a) A noun being used in a general sense will always take the definite article when it follows such verbs as **gustar** (to like), **preferir** (to prefer), **detestar** (to hate), **apreciar** (to appreciate), **respetar** (to respect), **rechazar** (to reject) and **combatir** (to combat).

   Prefiero el vino tinto. = I prefer red wine.

   Detesto el queso. = I hate cheese.

b) However, a noun being used in a general sense does not usually take the definite article when it follows such verbs as *comer* (to eat), *beber* (to drink), *tomar* (to drink, to take, to have), *consumir* (to consume), *usar* (to use), *utilizar* (to use), *emplear* (to use, to employ), *escribir* (to write), *fabricar* (to manufacture, to make), *producir* (to produce), *causar* (to cause), *querer* (to want), *desear* (to desire), *necesitar* (to need).

No tomo café, pero tomo té.
I don't drink coffee, but I drink tea.

Uso jabón normal en vez de champú para lavarme el pelo.
I use normal soap instead of shampoo to wash my hair.

c) If a noun has the idea of some/any, it does not take the definite article.

Tiene dinero.   = He's got money.

No tiene paciencia.   = He has no patience.

d) When **hay** means there is/are, the following noun does not take the definite article.

No hay disciplina en esta escuela.
There is no discipline in this school.

Hay gente buena y gente mala.
There are good people and bad people.

e) Be careful when using **prepositions**. Very often no definite article is needed with nouns being used in a general sense.

Él lo hace por amor, no por necesidad.
He does it for love, not through necessity.

¿Te imaginas una ciudad sin coches?
Can you imagine a city without cars.

Me trata con cariño.
He/she treats me with affection.

f) However, certain words always take the definite article (with or without a preposition):

*el colegio   el hospital   el trabajo   la universidad   la cárcel
la iglesia   la televisión   la natación   el tenis   las cartas* (and, indeed, all games and leisure activities).

Está en el colegio.   = He's at school.

Quiere ir a la universidad. = He wants to go to university.

Juego al tenis.   = I play tennis.

5.3 Masculine or feminine?

todos los problemas   un tema bastante complicado

- Most nouns that end in **-a** are feminine: *la vida, la escoba, la música*.

  There are, however, some important exceptions that you need to be aware of.

- Many (but not all) nouns that end in **-ma** are masculine. The most important of these are:

  el clima (climate); *el fantasma* (ghost); *el idioma* (language); *el poema* (poem); *el problema* (problem); *el programa* (programme); *el sistema* (system); *el telegrama* (telegram); *el tema* (theme/topic).

- Nouns that end in **-ista** may be either masculine or feminine, depending on the context.

  El/la turista (tourist); *el/la artista* (artist); *el/la dentista* (dentist); *el/la periodista* (journalist).

  Similarly, one can say *el/la atleta* (athlete).

- Special care should be taken with certain nouns ending in **-ía**.

el día	= the day
el tranvía	= the tram
el policía	= the policeman
la policía	= the police (force)/the policewoman
el/la espía	= the spy
el/la guía	= the guide (person)
la guía	= the guide book

- Other common masculine nouns ending in **-a** include:

  el guardarropa (wardrobe); *el mapa* (map); *el planeta* (planet); *el sofá* (sofa); *el vodka* (vodka).

- Most nouns that end in **-o** are masculine: *el río, el vino, el piano*.

  There are, however, a few feminine nouns that end in **-o**.

  la foto (photo); *la mano* (hand); *la moto* (motorbike); *la radio* (radio).

● For reasons of pronunciation, some words take **el** only in the singular form – even though these words are feminine.

el agua (water); *el hambre* (hunger); *el águila* (eagle); *el alma* (soul).

El agua está fría.   = The water is cold.

Las aguas del Mediterráneo = The waters of the Mediterranean

Practice (4): Distinguishing between masculine and feminine nouns

Complete each gap with **un** or **una**.

1 *Tenemos que comprar .... cama, ... guardarropa y .... sofá.*
2 *¿Puedo sacar .... foto?*
3 *¿Te apetece .... vodka o .... ginebra con limón?*
4 *No, no voy a escribirle .... carta. Voy a mandarle .... telegrama.*
5 *Saturno no es .... estrella, sino .... planeta que tiene unos anillos brillantes a su alrededor.*
6 *Van a presentar .... programa muy interesante a las ocho.*
7 *El inglés es .... idioma bastante complicado.*
8 *........ moto cuesta mucho más que .... bicicleta.*

Practice (5): Distinguishing between masculine and feminine nouns

Complete each gap with **el** or **la**.

1 *A veces escucho .... radio.*
2 *¿Por qué no miras ...... mapa que está en .... guía?*
3 *¿Cuál es .... tema de hoy?*
4 *Se estrecharon .... mano.*
5 *........ agua no está muy caliente.*
6 *¿Cuál es .... problema?*
7 *¿Quieres leer .... poema en voz alta?*
8 *Tienes que avisar a .... policía.*

5.4 Que or lo que?

los problemas sociales y económicos que España tiene
lo que sí veo...   lo que es verdaderamente triste es que...

● **Using que**

As a linking word, **que** (without an accent) has three basic meanings: **that/which/who**.

i) Joining a verb with a statement. (that)

Creo que han llegado.   = I think (that) they have arrived.

Dice que no quiere nada. = He says (that) he doesn't want anything.

In English **that** is optional after such verbs as *say, think, believe, think, promise, suggest.* In Spanish, however, **que** is obligatory when joining a verb with a statement.

Note that **Es que**... can be translated as **The fact is that**... .

Es que no tengo dinero. = The fact is that I don't have any money.

ii) Referring to a thing/object. (that/which)

Aquí está el libro que buscabas.
Here's the book (that/which) you were looking for.

Éstos no son los zapatos que quería.
These are not the shoes (that/which) I wanted.

Esa mesa, que es muy antigua, vale mucho dinero.
That table, which is very old, is worth a lot of money.

Again note that we can often omit **that/which** in English, but this is not the case in Spanish.

iii) Referring to a person. (who)

¿Conoces a aquella chica que nos está mirando?
Do you know that girl who is looking at us?

● **Using lo que**

As a linking phrase, **lo que** also has three basic meanings: **what/the thing that/which**.

i)   Joining a verb with an indirect question. (what)

  a) —*¿Qué ha pasado?* = What has happened? (*direct question*)
      —*No sé lo que ha pasado.* = I don't know what has happened.

  b) —*Qué vas a hacer?* = What are you going to do? (*direct question*)
      —*No sé lo que voy a hacer.* = I don't know what I'm going to do.

  NB: In the examples above, **qué** (with an accent) would also be correct.

  No sé qué ha pasado.   No sé qué voy a hacer.

  In other words, when joining a verb with an indirect question (what) you are free to choose between **lo que** or **qué**. There is, however, one exception. Before an infinitive, you must use **qué** and never **lo que**.

  No sé qué decir. = I don't know what to say.
  No sé qué hacer. = I don't know what to do.

ii) Linking a verb phrase with a statement. (what/the thing that)

  Lo que ha ocurrido es muy serio.
  What has happened is very serious.

  Lo que me extraña es su actitud. = The thing that surprises me is his attitude. / What I find odd is his attitude.

  Note the expression, **todo lo que…** (everything that…).

  Todo lo que has dicho es cierto. = Everything (that) you've said is true.

iii) Commenting on the preceding statement.   Commenting on a fact or idea that has just been expressed. (which)

  Pedro dice que no tiene dinero, lo que no es verdad
  Pedro says he has no money, which is not true.

  Luis no ha llamado, lo que me extraña porque siempre me llama antes de las ocho.
  Luis hasn't phoned, which I find odd because he always calls me before eight.

  In this particular context, you can use the slightly more formal **lo cual** instead of **lo que** if you so wish.

  Ella quiere dos mil pesetas por el reloj, lo cual me parece muy razonable.
  She wants 2000 pesetas for the watch, which seems very reasonable to me.

Practice (6): Recognising when to use **que** and **lo que**

Complete each gap with either **que** or **lo que**.

1 *El vestido .... has comprado te va muy bien.*

2 *¿Cómo se llama el señor .... vive en el quinto piso?*

3 *Te voy a explicar .... ha pasado.*

4 *Eso es precisamente .... nos hacía falta.*

5 *A mi parecer, ... hacen no es justo.*

6 *¿Qué dices? Es .... no entiendo .... estás diciendo.*

7 *La novela ....estoy leyendo es muy interesante.*

8 *Pedro no puede asistir a la reunión, ... es una lástima.*

9 *........ me fastidia es .... él nunca piensa en los demás.*

10 *Es verdad .... mucha gente hace todo .... puede para preservar a los animales de la extinción, pero .... es evidente también es .... en muchos casos ya es demasiado tarde.*

Extra reference

✦ A very useful phrase to know is the following: **Lo que pasa es que**...

(What's happening is that... / It's like this: / Well, actually...). This phrase is used to preface some sort of explanation.

Me gustaría ir contigo pero lo que pasa es que...
I would like to go with you, but the fact is ...

✦ Do not forget that **que** is used as a linking word with **sí** and **no**.

Claro que sí/claro que no	= Of course/of course not
Decir que sí/decir que no	= To say yes/to say no
Creer que sí/pensar que sí	= To believe so/to think so

✦ In colloquial speech, **que** is often placed in front of a short statement as a form of emphasis, as a shortened form of **es que** (the fact is that..) or as a shortened form of **porque** (because).

¡Que me voy!	= I'm off!
Que no me gusta, eso es todo.	= I just don't like it, that's all.
Cierra la puerta, ¡que hace frío!	= Shut the door – it's cold!

5.5 Choosing between **más que** and **más de**.

ha perdido más de lo que ha ganado

● **The problem of translating more than into Spanish**

Both **más que** and **más de** can be translated as **more than**. Study carefully the difference in usage between the two:

i) We usually use **más que** when making a comparison with a word that is not a verb.

Hoy hace más calor que ayer. = Today is hotter than yesterday.

Te quiero más que nunca. = I love you more than ever.

Pedro es más inteligente que yo. = Pedro is more intelligent than me.

ii) However, we use **más de** in front of a number or quantity/amount.

¡Has comido más de la mitad! = You've eaten more than half!

Son más de las siete. = It's gone seven. (It's later than seven o'clock.)

iii) We use **más de** + **lo que** when making a comparison with a verb phrase.

Es más rico de lo que parece. = He's richer than he appears.

Es más serio de lo que se cree. = It's more serious than people think.

iv) **Menos** follows the same basic pattern as **más**.

Yo gano menos que tú.   = I earn less than you (do).

Había menos de veinte personas. = There were fewer than twenty people.

Practice (7): Using **que** and **de** in comparative statements

Complete each statement with either **que** or **de**.

1 *Llevaba más .... un año sin saber nada de su mejor amigo.*

2 *El viaje duró más .... lo que esperábamos.*

3 *Tu trabajo es más fácil .... el mío.*

4 *Estoy cansado. He trabajado más .... doce horas.*

5 *Es mucho más inteligente .... lo que parece.*

6 *Hace más frío en el norte .... en el sur.*

7 *Él es más valiente .... lo que se cree.*

8 *El león mide más .... tres metros de largo y un metro de alto.*

9 *¿Crees que puedes hacerlo en menos .... diez minutos?*

10 *Tienes más paciencia .... yo.*

Extra reference

✦ Distinguishing between **más de lo que** and **más del que**

When making a comparison with a verb phrase, we usually use **más de lo que**. However, if a noun (rather than an adjective or adverb) is the actual focal point of comparison with a verb phrase, then we use **más + del que/de la que/de los que/de las que**.

Había más gente de la que se esperaba.
There were more people than expected.

✦ The difference between **más que** and **no ... más que**

Be careful not to confuse **más que** (more than) with **no ... más que** (only).

No piensa más que en comer y beber.
He only thinks about eating and drinking.

No tiene más que uno. = He's only got one.

5.6 Choosing between **pero** and **sino**.

no es la libertad sino el libertinaje   pero los cambios políticos...

● The problem of translating but into Spanish

Both **pero** and **sino** mean **but**. **Sino** contradicts a preceding statement, whereas **pero** is a normal conjunction linking one phrase with another. Look carefully at the following examples:

a) *Teresa ha llamado: no viene hoy, sino mañana.*
   Teresa phoned: she's not coming today but tomorrow.

Teresa ha llamado: no viene hoy, pero vendrá mañana.
Teresa phoned: she's not coming today, but she will come
tomorrow.

b) *No quiero éste, sino ése.*
I don't want this one but that one.

No me gusta éste, pero me gusta ése.
I don't like this one, but I like that one.

Note that **not only...but also** is translated as **no sólo...sino
también**.

No sólo toca la guitarra, sino el piano también.
Not only does he play the guitar, but the piano as well.

Practice (8): Distinguishing between sino and pero

Complete each gap with either **sino** or **pero**.

1 *No es español .... colombiano.*

2 *No hablo italiano, ... me defiendo en español.*

3 *No sólo habla italiano, ... español también.*

4 *No quería la camisa blanca, ... la amarilla.*

5 *No es muy inteligente, ... es honesto y de buen corazón.*

Extra reference

✦ Other meanings of **sino**

Sino can also mean **except** or **anything but**.

No quiere sino jugar. = He wants to do nothing but play.
(No quiere hacer más que jugar.)

✦ Distinguishing between **más** (more) and **mas** (but)

When you start to read Spanish literature, you will come across a
third word for *but*: **mas** (without an accent). This word is to be
found in literary Spanish and is rather archaic. While it is

important to recognise the word, do not use it in your own writing.

In the following extract from the Spanish novel "Tormento" by Benito Pérez Galdós, look at the way both **mas** and **sino** are used.

(Agustín Caballero is desperate to see the contents of two letters written by his fiancée, Amparo (Tormento). But the lady who has got these letters refuses to hand them over to him and, instead, throws them into the fire.)

Corrió Caballero a salvar del fuego lo que arrojara la endemoniada hembra; mas no llegó a tiempo. Las ascuas eran vivas, y el curioso no vio sino un papel que se retorcía y abarquillaba levantando tenue llama... Nada pudo leer sino un nombre que era la firma y decía: Tormento.

5.7 Recognising **dar** in idiomatic expressions.

podías dar un paseo   en eso te doy la razón

● **The problem of translating dar into English**

Just like **tener** and **hacer**, **dar** is an extremely versatile verb. The more Spanish you read, the more you will realise just how often **dar** is used in idiomatic expressions. Look carefully at the following examples:

dar un paseo (por el parque)	= to go for a walk (in the park)
dar un paseo en coche	= to go for a drive
dar una vuelta	= to go for a (short) walk
dar los buenos días/las buenas noches	= to say good morning/good night
dar las gracias	= to thank
dar la razón a uno	= to agree/concede that someone is right
darse cuenta (de que)	= to realise (that)
dar de comer a	= to feed
dar con alguien en la calle	= to run/bump into someone in the street

dar un disgusto a alguien	=	to upset/annoy/offend someone
dar asco	=	to disgust
dar una bofetada	=	to slap (across the face)
lo mismo me da/me da igual	=	it's all the same to me / I'm not bothered.
(porque) no me da la gana	=	(because) I don't feel like it / I don't want to. (Often said in a defiant/unpleasant tone of voice.)
me da rabia	=	it infuriates me/it makes me mad
me da vergüenza	=	I feel ashamed/embarrassed

Practice (9): Developing vocabulary in context

Use the following words to complete the dialogue below.

vergüenza   disgusto   cuenta   igual   gana   bofetada   rabia   vuelta

—*¿Adónde vas?*
—*Voy a dar una* .... (1).
—*Pero, hija, ¿vas a salir vestida así, con esa falda tan corta?*
¿No te da........? (2)
—*Pero, ¿por qué, mamá? Las mini-faldas están de moda.*
—*¿Qué va a pensar la gente? ¿Por qué no te pones algo más decente?*
—*A mí me da* .... (3) *la opinión de los demás.*
—*Ay, ¡qué* .... (4) *tan grande me estás dando, hija mía! ¿Cómo que no importa la opinión de los demás?*
—*Vamos, madre, no te pongas así. ¡No es para tanto!*
—*Cuando yo era joven, las chicas no andaban por las calles media desnudas.*

—*Los tiempos han cambiado, mamá. ¿No te has dado ....? (5)*
—*Yo soy tu madre y tienes que obedecerme.*
—*¿Y si no me da la ....? (6)*
—*¡Eso es lo que me da .... (7), tu insolencia! Siempre me llevas la contraria. Si sigues hablándome de esa manera, ¡te voy a dar una .... (8) bien fuerte, tú verás!*

Progress test 5

Translate the following into Spanish.

1 When she was younger, she used to go to church every Sunday.

2 At school I was afraid of certain teachers.

3 It was a lovely day. The sun was shining, the birds were singing and I felt really happy.

4 I don't like cats and I hate dogs.

5 Teachers do not earn a lot of money.

6 Sweets are bad for the teeth.

7 How many languages do you speak?

8 Can I take a photo?

9 I don't know what to do because I don't know what has happened.

10 What I want to know is why they have done that.

11 It is more difficult than people think.

12 He's not my son but my nephew!

13 It's all the same to me!

14 Do you want to go for a drive?

15 It disgusts me!

UNIT 6 Formal requests and relating past events

Mr Morales, a mild-mannered, middle-aged businessman, is sitting in his flat reading a newspaper. The door-bell rings. When he opens the door, four armed policemen burst in.

Policía 1: ¿Señor Morales?

Morales: Sí.

Policía 1: Policía! ¡No se mueva! ¡Las manos arriba!　　　　6.7

Morales: Pero…¿qué…?

Policía 2: ¡Cállese! ¡Haga lo que le decimos!　　　　6.7

Policía 1: Vamos al grano. ¿Dónde estuvo usted a las once　6.8
de esta mañana?

Morales: Yo no entiendo. Debe de haber alguna　　　　6.5
equivocación.

Policía 2: ¡Conteste! ¿Dónde estuvo usted esta mañana　6.7; 6.1
entre las once y las once y diez?

Morales:	Pues, a ver...No sé... <u>Salí</u> a dar una vuelta....	6.1
Policía 1:	¿A qué hora <u>salió</u> usted?	6.1
Morales:	Sobre las diez. <u>Di una vuelta</u> por la Plaza	6.1
	Mayor, <u>tomé un café</u> y después <u>fui al banco</u>...	6.1
Policía 1:	<u>Fue</u> usted al banco, ¿eh? ¿Para qué?	6.1
Morales:	Pues, lógicamente, para sacar dinero.	
Policía 1:	Para sacar dinero, ¿eh? Y, ¿cómo <u>sacó</u> usted este dinero?	6.1
Morales:	No entiendo la pregunta.	
Policía 1:	<u>Quiero que conteste.</u> ¿Cómo sacó usted el dinero?	6.6
Morales:	Bueno, <u>me acerqué</u> a la caja, <u>presenté un cheque</u> y...	6.1
Policía 2:	Ha olvidado usted un pequeño detalle. <u>¿No tenía usted una pistola</u> en la mano cuando se acercó a la caja?	6.2
Morales:	¿Una pistola? ¿Yo? ¡Dios mío!	
Policía 1:	<u>Empecemos desde el principio,</u> y esta vez <u>quiero que usted nos diga la verdad.</u>	6.8 6.6
Morales:	¿Puedo saber de qué me acusan?	
Policía 2:	<u>Hubo un atraco</u> en el banco de Bilbao a eso de las once de esta mañana. <u>Al salir corriendo del banco,</u> el atracador <u>dejó caer</u> este sobre. ¿Lo reconoce? Lleva su nombre y esta dirección.	6.1 6.3/6.4 6.1
Morales:	¿Me permite verlo?	
Policía 2:	Aquí está. <u>Mire.</u> Y ahora, ¿qué tiene usted que decir?	6.7
Morales:	Bueno, aquí pone "apartamento 6". Yo vivo en el número cinco. <u>Miren ustedes</u> la puerta. Y mi vecino, que es un tipo algo extraño, también se llama Morales. Además, éste <u>salió de su apartamento hace diez minutos. Llevaba una maleta y tenía mucha prisa.</u>	6.7 6.2 6.2 6.2
Policía 1:	¡********! ¡Vámonos, muchachos!	6.8

6.1 Forming and using the Preterite.

¿Dónde estuvo usted...? salí salió di una vuelta
tomé un café fui al banco fue sacó me acerqué
presenté un cheque hubo un atraco dejó caer.

- **The function(s) of the Preterite tense in Spanish**

  The Preterite tense in Spanish is equivalent to the Past Simple narrative tense in English ("I came, I saw, I conquered").

  i) Just as in English, the Preterite is used to show completed action at a particular moment in the past.

  En cuanto me vio, empezó a correr hacia la salida.
  As soon as he saw me, he started to run towards the exit.

  ii) When referring to a period of time, the Preterite gives an immediate picture of completion (something started and finished within a clearly defined time framework).

  Estuvo dos meses en España y luego fue a Francia.
  He was in Spain for two months and then went to France.

  iii) Just as in English we use the Past Simple to interrupt a background description supplied by the past continuous tense ("I was having a bath when the telephone rang."), so too in Spanish the Preterite is used to interrupt the Imperfect/Imperfect Continuous tense ("*Estaba tomando un baño cuando sonó el teléfono*").

  Yo salía de la casa cuando recordé que...
  I was going out of the house when I remembered that...

- **Forming the Preterite.**

  i) -AR verbs: Remove the **-ar** from the infinitive and add **-é, -aste, -ó, -amos, -asteis, -aron.** (Note the accents on the first and third persons singular.)

  contar: conté, contaste, contó, contamos, contasteis, contaron.

ii) -ER/-IR verbs: Remove the **-er** / **-ir** from the infinitive and add **-í, -iste, -ió, -imos, -isteis, -ieron.**

romper: rompí, rompiste, rompió, rompimos, rompisteis, rompieron.

salir: salí, saliste, salió, salimos, salisteis, salieron.

(Again, note the accents on the first and third persons singular.)

iii) Spelling changes.

The following spelling rules apply when forming the Preterite:

a) Before **i** and **e, z** becomes **c.**

empezar: empecé, empezaste, empezó, empezamos, empezasteis, empezaron.

cruzar: crucé, cruzaste, cruzó, cruzamos, cruzasteis, cruzaron.

b) Before **i** and **e**, a hard **g** becomes **gu.**

llegar: llegué, llegaste, llegó, llegamos, llegasteis, llegaron.

pagar: pagué, pagaste, pagó, pagamos, pagasteis, pagaron.

c) Before **e**, a hard **c** becomes **qu.**

sacar: saqué, sacaste, sacó, sacamos, sacasteis, sacaron.

d) A soft, unaccented **i** between two vowels becomes **y.**

oír: oí, oíste, oyó, oímos, oísteis, oyeron.

caer: caí, caíste, cayó, caímos, caísteis, cayeron.

iv) Radical-changing -IR verbs.

These can be very confusing, and so particular attention should be paid to their formation. The Preterite of radical-changing -IR verbs is formed in the same way as for normal -IR verbs, except for the third person (singular/plural) when **e** becomes **i** and **o** becomes **u.**

seguir: seguí, seguiste, siguió, seguimos, seguisteis, siguieron.

sentir: sentí, sentiste, sintió, sentimos, sentisteis, sintieron.

dormir: dormí, dormiste, durmió, dormimos, dormisteis, durmieron.

v) Irregular verbs (1).

a) **Ser** and **Ir** have the same Preterite form:

fui, fuiste, fue, fuimos, fuisteis, fueron. (Note: no accents.)
Pedro fue a verla. = Pedro went to see her.
Fue Pedro quien me lo contó. = It was Pedro who told me.

b) *dar: di, diste, dio, dimos, diste, dieron.* (Note: no accents.)

ver: vi, viste, vio, vimos, viste, vieron. (Note: no accents.)

When you start reading Spanish literature written before 1959, you will find that these particular verbs used to carry accents (eg: *fué; dió; vió*). This is no longer the case.

vi) Irregular verbs (2) : The **pretérito grave**.

The following verbs are all irregular, but follow the same pattern of irregularity (which is why they are all grouped together under the umbrella term, **pretérito grave**). When learning these verbs by heart, there are four things you should bear in mind:

a) There are no accents on these verbs.

b) The endings of these verbs are **-e, -iste, -o, -imos, -isteis, -ieron**.

c) If the stem of the verb is **j, -ieron** becomes **-eron**.

d) The stem of these verbs does not change in the Preterite. So, all you need to learn is the Ist person singular of each verb – and then add the appropriate ending within context.

i)

Estar	Haber	Saber	Poner	Andar
estuve	hube	supe	puse	anduve
estuviste	hubiste	supiste	pusiste	anduviste
estuvo	hubo	supo	puso	anduvo
estuvimos	hubimos	supimos	pusimos	anduvimos
estuvisteis	hubisteis	supisteis	pusisteis	anduvisteis
estuvieron	hubieron	supieron	pusieron	anduvieron

Poder	Querer	Tener	Venir
pude	quise	tuve	vine
pudiste	quisiste	tuviste	viniste
pudo	quiso	tuvo	vino
pudimos	quisimos	tuvimos	vinimos
pudisteis	quisisteis	tuvisteis	vinisteis
pudieron	quisieron	tuvieron	vinieron

ii)

Conducir	Producir	Decir	Traer
conduje	*produje*	*dije*	*traje*
condujiste	*produjiste*	*dijiste*	*trajiste*
condujo	*produjo*	*dijo*	*trajo*
condujimos	*produjimos*	*dijimos*	*trajimos*
condujisteis	*produjisteis*	*dijisteis*	*trajisteis*
condujeron	*produjeron*	*dijeron*	*trajeron*

NB: Be careful with **hacer**. To retain the original sound of the verb, the stem of the third person singular changes from **c** to **z**.

hacer: hice, hiciste, hizo, hicimos, hicisteis, hicieron.

Finally, note that the Preterite of **hay** is **hubo** (there was/were).

Practice (1): Using the preterite to relate events in the past

Change each verb in brackets into an appropriate form of the Preterite.

Día negro en Madrid:
dos accidentes espectaculares provocan dos muertos

Ayer (ser) un día negro en Madrid por dos siniestros que, por su espectacularidad, (mover) a numerosos policías, bomberos y sanitarios.

Uno de ellos (ser) un incendio en el barrio de Salamanca, y el otro la caída de un automóvil al río Manzanares. En ambos sucesos (registrarse) víctimas mortales y, además, (provocar) cortes de tráfico.

El incendio (comenzar) poco antes del mediodía, en el número 58 de la calle Juan Bravo. En él (perecer) una mujer.

El portero del inmueble realizaba su trabajo habitual cuando (ver) cómo de una de las viviendas del cuarto piso salía una gran humareda. Por ello, (subir) hasta el lugar de donde procedía el incendio y, tras comprobar que no contestaba nadie, (dar) parte a los bomberos.

Cuando los miembros de los equipos contraincendios (entrar) en el piso (hallar) a su inquilina muerta, María Isabel Perdigón González, de 50 años, quien, al parecer, (perecer) por inhalación de humo.

El otro accidente (ocurrir) una hora antes cuando un turismo (precipitarse), por causas aún desconocidas, al Manzanares. El conductor, Andrés Moreno Mínguez, policía municipal, (ser) rescatado por un hombre llamado Adolfo, quien le (trasladar) al Hospital Doce de Octubre, donde posteriormente (fallecer). La intervención del Grupo Subacuático de los bomberos para rescatar el vehículo, (provocar), igualmente, grandes atascos.

Practice (2): Further practice in the formation and use of the preterite

Change each verb in brackets into an appropriate form of the Preterite.

APARECE AHORCADO BUSTER EDWARDS,
uno de los 15 autores del asalto al tren de Glasgow

Londres. Buster Edwards, uno de los 15 autores del legendario robo del tren de Glasgow, (aparecer) ayer ahorcado en un garaje detrás del puesto de flores que tenía en la estación londinense de Waterloo. El ex delincuente ya había intentado suicidarse anteriormente con una sobredosis de pastillas para dormir y con paracetamol

El cadáver de Edwards (ser) descubierto muerto por su hermano Terence al mediodía de ayer. Los médicos (acudir) inmediatamente, pero todos los esfuerzos para reanimarlo (resultar) infructuosos. La policía ha dicho que no hay elementos sospechosos y que, a falta de la autopsia, todo apunta al suicidio.

Buster Edwards, que tenía 62 años, (repartirse) en 1963 con los otros miembros de la banda la nada despreciable cifra de dos millones y medio de libras esterlinas -unos quinientos millones de pesetas-, que en aquella época (conseguir) batir todos los records de botines conseguidos en robos.

El 8 de agosto de 1963 Buster y compañía (ejecutar) a la perfección su largamente elaborado plan. Como si se tratara de una película del Oeste (instalar) una señal falsa de alto en la vía por la que circulaba un tren correo, en el llamado Cruce de Sears, cerca de la localidad de Chaddington (Buckinghamshire), y (apoderarse) de todo el dinero que llevaba a bordo.

En el juicio, que (llevarse) a cabo dos años más tarde, todos los implicados (ser) declarados culpables y condenados a treinta años de prisión.

La vida de Edwards (inspirar) en 1988 la película "Buster", protagonizada por el cantante Phil Collins y que (popularizar) el tema del intérprete "Two hearts", dos corazones.

Extra reference

✦ The position of pronouns with the preterite (the difference between standard Spanish and literary Spanish):

Just as with the Present tense, any pronoun is normally positioned in front of a verb in the preterite.

Me dijo. = He said to me.

Se volvió. = He turned round.

Se levantó. = He got up.

When you start reading Spanish literature, you will find that some authors attach the pronoun to the end of the verb in the preterite: *volvióse, levantóse.*

While it is important for you to recognise this literary form, do not use it in your own writing.

6.2 Distinguishing between the Preterite and the Imperfect.

¿No tenía usted una pistola cuando...? salió de su
apartamento hace diez minutos llevaba una maleta y tenía
mucha prisa

● **The problem of translating from English into Spanish when referring to the past**

In English the past simple can be used both as a past narrative tense (the Preterite in Spanish) and as a past descriptive tense (the Imperfect in Spanish). This means, for example, that **he had** can be translated as either **tuvo** or **tenía** depending on the context. Or **he worked** can be translated as **trabajó** or **trabajaba** depending on the context.

To avoid possible confusion, it is important to understand the broad differences between the two tenses. Before studying the guidelines below, look again at sections 5.1 (the Imperfect) and 6.1 (the Preterite).

● **Summarising the essential functions of the Preterite and the Imperfect, and illustrating the fundamental differences between the two tenses**

i) Completed action – even though the action may have occurred over a period of time – is shown by the Preterite.

Tuve un examen ayer. = I had an exam yesterday.

Pasó un año en España. = He spent a year in Spain.

but

Yo estaba nervioso porque tenía un examen.
I was nervous because I had an exam. (Open-ended description in the past.)

Siempre pasaba las vacaciones en España.
He always spent his holidays in Spain. (Habitual action in the past.)

ii) Completed action at a particular moment of time is shown by the Preterite, even though the verb may seem to be descriptive.

Fue en aquel momento en que me di cuenta de lo que pasaba.
It was at that moment that I realised what was happening.

but

En aquel momento me di cuenta de que no era el momento de decirle la verdad.
At that moment I realised that it was not the moment to tell him the truth.

iii Even if the verb appears to be descriptive, the Preterite is used if the verb clearly refers to a complete period of time in the past (ie: the limits are defined).

Ayer estuve en casa todo el día. = Yesterday I was at home all day.

Estuvo enfermo durante tres meses. = He was ill for three months.

but

Yo estaba en casa cuando oí la noticia.
I was at home when I heard the news.

Mi padre estaba tan enfermo que casi no podía hablar.
My father was so ill that he could hardly speak.

iv) As a rule of thumb, verbs expressing emotions, knowledge and belief tend to be used more often in the Imperfect.

Yo sospechaba que ella ya no me quería.
I suspected that she no longer loved me.

Yo sabía que él no creía en Dios.
I knew that he didn't believe in God.

v) The Imperfect is used to establish the background or set the scene in the past. This includes stating the time in the past.

Eran las diez cuando salí de la casa.
It was ten o'clock when I left the house.

vi) Be especially careful when using the past participle with either **ser** or **estar.**

Estaban sentados a la mesa cuando fueron atacados.
They were sitting at the table (description in the past) when they were attacked (action, passive).

Practice (3): Recognising when to use the Preterite and the Imperfect

Complete the following three jokes by changing each verb in brackets into the correct form of either the Preterite or Imperfect.

a) *Sánchez (ser) un jugador empedernido que (apostar) dinero en cuanto (poder): caballos, perros, quinielas, dados, dominó y juegos de naipes.*

Un día (jugar) a las cartas con González, cuando éste (morir) de repente. Sánchez (ser) el encargado de darle la noticia a la señora de González.

Ésta le (abrir) en cuanto (llamar) a la puerta.

—Perdone —dijo Sánchez—. ¿Es usted la viuda de González?

—Yo no soy viuda.

—¿Le importaría apostar algo, señora?

b) *Marcelino (casarse) con una mujer muy guapa. Para conservarse así, todas las noches ella (ponerse) crema en la cara y (untarse) el cuerpo con aceites. Esto (ser) la causa del fracaso amoroso de Marcelino. Cada vez que (tratar) de abrazarla, su mujer (salir) disparada por la ventana.*

c) *El paciente (estar) convencido de haberse tragado un caballo. Nada de cuanto le (decir) el psiquiatra (poder) hacerle cambiar de idea.*

Desesperado, el doctor le (poner) una inyección que le (dejar) profundamente dormido. Cuando el paciente (despertar), el psiquiatra (hallarse) junto a su cama sosteniendo por la brida a un hermoso caballo gris.

—*iYa no tiene que preocuparse!* —*dijo*—. *Le hemos operado y le hemos extraído el caballo. ¿Verdad que es precioso?*
—*¿A quién trata de engañar?* —*(exclamar) el paciente*—. *El que yo (tragarse) (ser) un caballo negro.*

Extra reference

Certain verbs have an extra meaning when used in the preterite. Look carefully at the following examples:

No quería hacerlo	=	He didn't want to do it.
No quiso hacerlo.	=	He refused to do it.
La conocía.	=	I knew her.
La conocí en Madrid.	=	I met her in Madrid.
Yo sabía la verdad.	=	I knew the truth.
Cuando supe la verdad,	=	When I found out the truth,...

6.3 Using **al** + infinitive.

al salir corriendo del banco

● A very useful construction to know is **al** + infinitive, which is equivalent to the "on doing…" (when/as…) construction in English.

Al salir del banco, dejó caer un sobre.
As he left the bank, he dropped an envelope.

Al verme, rompió a llorar.
On seeing me, she burst into tears.

Practice (4): Becoming familiar with the use of **al** + infinitive

Match items 1–8 with items a–h

1   *Al darme cuenta del error,*

2   *Al oír los gritos,*

3   *Al salir del supermercado, yo*

4   *Al ver a su padre,*

5 *Al bajar las escaleras, Pedro*
6 *Al descubrir la verdad, Consuelo*
7 *Al llegar a la estación,*
8 *Al abrir el cajón,*

a *me encontré con Rocío.*
b *fuimos directamente al andén número 5.*
c *se resbaló y se cayó.*
d *descubrió que el dinero no estaba allí.*
e *volví inmediatamente a la tienda.*
f *se asomó a la ventana para ver qué pasaba.*
g *se puso furiosa.*
h *el niño dejó de llorar.*

Extra reference

✦ Time phrases with **a**

The preposition **a** is used in many time phrases. Look very carefully at the following examples, noting in particular the use of **al**.

i) *Al día siguiente, nos pusimos en marcha.*
The following day we set off.

Al poco rato, Miguel volvió.
Shortly afterwards, Miguel returned.

Llegaron al anochecer.
They arrived at nightfall.

Al mediodía…
At mid-day…

ii) *A principios de noviembre se mudó de casa.*
At the beginning of November he moved house.

A mediados de agosto….
In the middle of August…

A fines de marzo…
At the end of March…

iii) *A los cinco minutos estaba dormido.*
Within five minutes he was asleep.

A los ocho años, José...
When he was eight, José...

iv) *A la semana siguiente...*
The following week...

La pobre mujer murió a la semana del accidente.
The poor woman died a week after the accident.

✦ Developing vocabulary: common time phrases

Not all time phrases, of course, take **a**. Look at the following common time phrases:

hace un año	=	a year ago
hace poco	=	not long ago
el año pasado	=	last year
la semana pasada	=	last week

6.4 Verb + **corriendo**   *(reference only)*

al salir corriendo del banco

● The problem of translating such phrases as **run out**, **run down** and **run back**

In English we add a preposition to the verb **run** when we wish to show direction.

eg He ran out of the bank. He ran down the street. He ran back.

In Spanish the emphasis is different.

i) *Salió del banco.*   = He came out of the bank.
   Salió corriendo del banco. = He ran out of the bank.

ii) *Bajó por la calle.*   = He went down the street.
    Bajó corriendo por la calle. = He ran down the street.

iii) *Volvió.*   = He came/went back.
     Volvió corriendo.   = He ran back.

6.5 deber or deber de?

debe de haber alguna equivocación

- **The basic meanings of must in English and deber in Spanish**

  In English **must** has two basic meanings:

  You must do it. (*obligation*)   = You have to do it.
  He must be rich. (*assumption*)   = I am sure he is rich.

  In Spanish **deber** also has two basic meanings. When **deber** implies obligation, it never takes **de**. When **deber** expresses an assumption, it usually takes **de** – but it can be omitted if you so wish. Look carefully at the following examples:

  i) Obligation

  Debes tratarle con más respeto.
  You must treat him with more respect.

  Debo regresar a mi país.
  I must return to my country.

  ii) Assumption

  No has desayunado ni almorzado. ¡Debes (de) tener hambre!
  You haven't had breakfast nor lunch. You must be hungry!

  ¡Debes (de) tener frío!
  You must be cold!

Practice (5): Understanding the underlying meaning of **deber** in context

In which of the following sentences can we put in **de** after **deber** in order to show more clearly that it is expressing an assumption?

1 *Debemos marcharnos.*

2 *No debes comer tanto chocolate.*

3 *Debe ser interesante ser modelo.*

4 *¿No ha llegado todavía? ¡Debes estar preocupada!*

5 *Debemos levantarnos temprano mañana.*

6 *Debe haber alguna razón por la cual no ha llamado.*

7 *Ah, usted debe ser el marido de Angelita.*

8 *Debemos decírselo cuanto antes.*

9 *Consuelo parece muy preocupada últimamente. Debe tener algún problema. ¿Quieres hablar con ella?*

10 *El médico me dijo que debía dejar de fumar.*

6.6 Introducing the Present Subjunctive

quiero que conteste   quiero que usted nos diga la verdad

● **What is the subjunctive?**

The Spanish language has two moods: the Indicative and the Subjunctive.

Both moods are expressed through verbs in the appropriate tense. In the first five units of this book, we have been using the Indicative only.

● **What is the difference between the Indicative mood and the Subjunctive mood?**

In very broad terms, we can say that the Indicative mood deals with what is real and existing (concrete facts and real possibilities), whereas the Subjunctive mood focuses on either hypothetical situations (imagining and supposing) or on things that are not yet certain.

Another way of looking at the two moods is to think of the Indicative as focusing on something definite, whereas the Subjunctive is more indefinite.

● **Does the Subjunctive mood express anything else?**

In addition to the above, we need to remember that the Subjunctive is the voice of command and strong suggestion.

● **Does the Subjunctive exist in English?**

In English we have more or less dropped the use of the Subjunctive, although it still exists in such phrases as "If I were you, I would.." ("I'm not you, but let's imagine that I am.") or "I wish I didn't have to go to school" ("I have to go to school, but it would be nice if I didn't have to.").

● Forming the Present Subjunctive

i) **-AR verbs**

Remove the **-o** of the first person singular of the Present tense Indicative and add **-e, -es, -e, -emos, -éis, -en**.

Hablar	Encontrar
hable	*encuentre*
hables	*encuentres*
hable	*encuentre*
hablemos	*encontremos*
habléis	*encontréis*
hablen	*encuentren*

Note that radical-changing verbs follow the same pattern of change in both the Present Subjunctive and Indicative.

ii) **-ER and -IR verbs**

Remove the **-o** of the first person singular of the Present tense Indicative and add **-a, -as, -a, -amos, -áis, -an**.

Comer	Entender	Salir
coma	*entienda*	*salga*
comas	*entiendas*	*salgas*
coma	*entienda*	*salga*
comamos	*entendamos*	*salgamos*
comáis	*entendáis*	*salgáis*
coman	*entiendan*	*salgan*

iii) **Irregular**

In a very few cases, the first person singular of the Present tense Indicative does not end in **-o**. These verbs need to be learnt separately.

Dar	Estar	Haber	Ir	Saber	Ser
dé	esté	haya	vaya	sepa	sea
des	estés	hayas	vayas	sepas	seas
dé	esté	haya	vaya	sepa	sea
demos	estemos	hayamos	vayamos	sepamos	seamos
déis	estéis	hayáis	vayáis	sepáis	seáis
den	estén	hayan	vayan	sepan	sean
(Note the accents)	(Note the accents)	(Subjunctive of 'hay' = haya)			

iv) **Spelling changes**

a) Pay special attention to -AR verbs that end in **-car, -gar**, or **-zar**. In the present subjunctive these verbs will end in **-que, -gue**, or **-ce**.

tocar (toque); sacar (saque); pagar (pague); colgar (cuelgue); empezar (empiece); cruzar (cruce).

b) For -ER and -IR verbs, any spelling change in the first person singular of the present tense indicative is retained in the present subjunctive.

conocer (conozca); coger (coja); seguir (siga).

● **Using the Present Subjunctive with indirect wishes, requests and commands.**

In English we use the Infinitive after such verbs as **wish, want, ask** and **tell** irrespective of whether there is a change of subject in the second part of the sentence. In Spanish, however, **que** + the Subjunctive must be used if there is a change of subject in the second half of the sentence.

Look very carefully at the following examples:

I want to go there. = *Quiero ir allí.* (infinitive)

I want you to go there. = *Quiero que (tú) vayas allí.* (subjunctive)

They want to learn French.   = *Quieren aprender francés.*
                                                 (infinitive)
They want me to learn French. = *Quieren que (yo) aprenda francés.*

Practice (6): Recognising when to use the Present Subjunctive (indirect wishes and requests)

Change each verb in brackets into the correct form of the Present Subjunctive if necessary. Simply tick the sentence if no change is required.

1 *Ella quiere que yo (cambiar) de trabajo.*

2 *Ella quiere (cambiar) de trabajo.*

3 *No quiero (salir) esta noche.*

4 *No quiero que tú (salir) esta noche.*

5 *Mi padre quiere (comprar) otro coche.*

6 *¿Quieres que yo te (comprar) algo?*

7 *¿Qué quieres (hacer)?*

8 *¿Qué quieres que (hacer) yo?*

9 *Voy a pedirle que me (escribir) más a menudo.*

10 *¿Por qué no le pides a Teresa que te (ayudar)?*

11 *Dígale a Pedro que me (llamar) mañana.*

12 *Dígales a sus hermanos que (venir) mañana.*

6.7 Using the Formal Imperative (**usted/ustedes**)

¡No se mueva!   ¡Cállese! ¡Haga..!   ¡Conteste!   Mire Miren ustedes

---

● What is the Formal Imperative?

When you are addressing one or more people in a formal manner and you are giving direct instructions/orders or making some kind of direct request, you need to use the Formal Imperative.

● **Forming the Formal Imperative**

The Formal Imperative is formed by the third person (singular/plural) of the present subjunctive.

¡Conteste!	= Answer! (*talking to one person*)
¡Contesten!	= Answer! (*talking to more than one person*)
Pase(n), por favor.	= Please come in.
¡Abra(n) la maleta!	= Open the suitcase!
No sea(n) tan impaciente(s).	= Don't be so impatient.

● **Using pronouns with the Formal Imperative**

If a pronoun is used with an Imperative, the pronoun is added to the Imperative (but not if the Imperative is negative). When a pronoun is added to an Imperative, an accent is usually required to indicate where the stress is.

Póngalo aquí.	= Put it here.
No lo ponga en la mesa.	= Don't put it on the table.
Siéntese, por favor.	= Sit down, please.
¡No se siente allí!	= Don't sit there!

Practice (7): Using the Formal Imperative in context

Change each verb in brackets into a formal imperative. In each case, use the singular form (**usted**).

1 —*(Oír).*
—*(Decirme).*
—*¿Está Manuel?*
—*¿De parte de quién?*

2 —*(Perdonar), señor. ¿Por dónde se va al hotel Sol y Sombra?*
—*(Bajar) por esta calle y (tomar) la primera a la derecha.*
—*Gracias.*
—*De nada.*

3 —*¿Me puede decir dónde está Correos, por favor?*
—*Sí, (mirar). (Subir) por aquí, (seguir) todo recto y (coger) la segunda a la izquierda.*
—*Gracias.*
—*No hay de qué.*

4 —*Entonces, ¿qué me aconseja?*
—*No (trabajar) tanto y (tratar) de relajar. Sobre todo, (hacer) más ejercicio y (dejar) de fumar.*
—*¿Y las pastillas?*
—*(Seguir) tomando las mismas pastillas y (volver) en ocho días.*

5 —*Me duele mucho el pie. Casi no puedo caminar.*
—*(Quedarse) en la cama por unos cuantos días y (tomar) esta medicina tres veces al día. (Agitar) la botella antes de usarla.*

6 —*¡No (enfadarse) usted!*
—*¡(Salir) de aquí! ¡(Marcharse)! ¡(Irse) inmediatamente!*
—*¡(Calmarse), por favor!... ¡(Oír)! ¡No me (empujar)!*

6.8 Translating **Let's...**   *(reference only)*

**Vamos al grano.   Empecemos desde el principio.
¡Vámonos, muchachos!**

● The first person plural (**-emos/-amos**) of the present subjunctive is used when you wish to make a suggestion that is either fairly urgent or to be acted upon immediately.

Hablemos de otra cosa.	= Let's talk about something else.
Cambiemos de tema.	= Let's change the subject.
¡Sentémosnos aquí!	= Let's sit down here.
Abramos una ventana.	= Let's open a window.

The one exception is the verb **ir**, where the indicative form is usually retained for direct suggestions.

-¿Queréis ir al cine?	= Do you want to go to the cinema?
-Sí, ¡vamos!	= Yes, let's go!

Likewise, the indicative form is also used for **irse: ¡Vámonos!**

This does not mean to say that the subjunctive form of **vamos** is never used. When using particular fixed phrases, some Spanish speakers prefer **vayamos** to **vamos**. For example, there is nothing wrong with saying (rather formally) *"¡Vayamos al grano!"* (Let's get to the point!) instead of *"¡Vamos al grano!"*. However, as a general rule, you should avoid **vayamos** when speaking or writing Spanish, since it will usually sound old-fashioned and rather stilted.

● You do not have to use the Subjunctive to translate **Let's...** Instead, you can use **Vamos a** + Infinitive. This construction is more casual, more general and usually less urgent than the subjunctive form.

Vamos a ver,...   = Let's see,...

Vamos a hablar de otra cosa. = Let's talk about something else.

Progress test 6

Translate the following into Spanish.

1   He said he had a headache and wasn't feeling very well.

2   The following day they got up very early.

3   Last year I went to Spain and spent two weeks in Huelva.

4   We were in Spain for five months and then we went to France.

5   She explained that she was very tired and wanted to rest.

6   When did you meet her? Two or three years ago?

7   He ran out of the house.

8   On seeing me, he smiled and shook my hand.

9   They want me to start tomorrow.

10   What do they want us to do?

11   I want you to open your suitcase! (*formal situation, one to one*)

12   Look at it, but don't touch it. (*formal situation, one to one. Use **lo** for it.*)

13   Come in. Sit down, please. (*formal situation, one to one.*)

14   She must be hungry.

15   Let's start from the beginning!

UNIT 7 Informal instructions and referring to the future

José and Lola are on board a plane. This is the first time Lola has flown and she is hating every minute of it.

Lola: Creo que me voy a desmayar.

José: Toma este coñac, te hará bien.   7.1; 7.2

Lola: Gracias… Para mí este vuelo es una verdadera pesadilla. No puedo relajarme.

José: ¿Quieres que hable con la azafata?

Lola: No, no quiero molestar. Aguantaré hasta que   7.2/7.3
lleguemos. Pero, te digo una cosa, la próxima vez
viajaremos en tren, por mucho que dure el viaje. Es   7.2
que me siento asfixiada dentro de un avión. Y
tengo miedo. Tengo este presentimiento…

José: ¡No seas boba! No va a pasar nada.   7.1

Lola: Espero que no… Ya vuelvo. Voy al baño.

José: Mira. Cuando vuelvas te voy a enseñar un truco   7.1; 7.3
con cartas, para que te distraigas. ¿Vale?   7.4

Lola: Vale.

(Cinco minutos más tarde, Lola ha vuelto y José ha sacado una baraja de cartas)

José: ¿Te sientes mejor?

Lola: Sí, gracias. Estoy un poquito más relajada.

José: Bueno, ahora <u>te enseñaré</u> un truco. <u>Escoge una</u>   7.2; 7.1
<u>carta</u> de esta baraja. <u>No me la enseñes,</u> y <u>vuelve a</u>   7.6; 7.1
<u>meterla</u> en el montón. Ahora voy a barajar las
cartas y <u>sacaré</u> la misma carta que tú escogiste.   7.2

Lola: ¡A ver!

José: ¡Aquí! Mira. ¿Es ésta la carta que escogiste?

Lola: Sí,... pero....

José: ¿Qué pasa, Lola? <u>¡Te has puesto muy pálida!</u>   7.5

Lola: Esa carta. La que tienes en la mano. <u>¡Mírala!</u> ¡Mira   7.1
el número! ¡Mira el color!

José: ¿Qué? No entiendo. ¿Por qué estás temblando?

Lola: Dicen que esa carta trae mala suerte. Significa la
muerte. ¡Ay, Dios mío! ¡Me voy a desmayar!

7.1 Forming and using the Informal Imperative

**Toma este coñac ¡No seas boba! Mira Escoge una carta
...y vuelve a meterla ¡Mírala!**

- **What is the Informal Imperative?**

In the conversation, José and Lola are friends. Naturally, they use the
tú form when addressing each other. When asking or telling the
other to do something, they use the Informal Imperative.

- **Forming the Informal Imperative**

The positive and negative forms of the Informal Imperative need to
be learnt separately.

● **Positive form**

i) Regular verbs:

a) The majority of verbs, including radical-changing ones, are regular.

b) The singular form (**tú**) of the Informal Imperative has the same form as the third person singular of the Present tense (Indicative). This is particularly important to remember when dealing with radical-changing verbs.

c) The plural form (**vosotros/as**) is formed by changing the final **-r** of the Infinitive to **-d**. This rule applies to radical-changing verbs as well.

	singular (tú)	**plural (vosotros/as)**
Hablar:	*habla*	*hablad*
Contar(ue):	*cuenta*	*contad*
Beber:	*bebe*	*bebed*
Volver(ue):	*vuelve*	*volved*
Vivir:	*vive*	*vivid*
Pedir(i):	*pide*	*pedid*

Habla(d) más despacio, por favor.   = Speak more slowly, please.

¡Vuelve/Volved pronto!   = Come back soon!

ii) Irregular verbs:

	singular (tú)	**plural (vosotros/as)**
Decir:	*di*	*decid*
Hacer:	*haz*	*haced*
Ir:	*ve*	*id*
Poner:	*pon*	*poned*
Salir:	*sal*	*salid*
Ser:	*sé*	*sed*
Tener:	*ten*	*tened*
Venir:	*ven*	*venid*

Ven aquí, Rosita. = Come here, Rosita.

Venid aquí, niños. = Come here, children.

¡Sé bueno! = Be good!

¡Sal de aquí! = Get out of here!

iii) Reflexive verbs and object pronouns:

In the positive form, any object or reflexive pronoun is added to the imperative form (and the rules of accentuation apply).

levantarse:

¡Levántate! (tú) = Get up!

¡Levantaos! (vosotros/as) Note that the **-d** is dropped before **-os**.

sentarse:

¡Siéntate! (tú) = Sit down!

¡Sentaos! (vosotros/as)

irse:

¡Vete! (tú) = Go away!

¡Idos! (vosotros/as) Note that, in the case of **Ir** only, the **-d** is not dropped before **-os**.

hacer + lo: ¡Hazlo! (tú)	=	Do it!
pedir + le: ¡Pídele! (tú)	=	Ask him!
abrir + lo: ¡Abridlo! (vosotros/as)	=	Open it!
dar + le: ¡Dadle algo! (vosotros/as)	=	Give him something!

● Negative form

The negative of the Informal Imperative is formed by the **tú** and **vosotros/as** forms of the Present Subjunctive. This applies to all verbs. There are no exceptions.

Any reflexive or object pronoun is kept in front of the verb; it is never added to a negative imperative.

¡No lo compres! (¡No lo compréis!) = Don't buy it.

¡No lo toques! (¡No lo toquéis!) = Don't touch it.

¡No te vayas! (¡No os vayáis!) = Don't go (away).

Practice (1): Telling one person or more to do something

For the following verbs, give both the **tú** form (positive) and the **vosotros/as** form (positive) of the Informal Imperative.

eg *Empujar: ¡Empuja! ¡Empujad!*

1 *Tirar:*   ....

2 *Empezar:*   ....

3 *Pensar:*   ....

4 *Correr:*   ....

5 *Volver:*   ....

6 *Tener:*   ....

7 *Escribir:*   ....

8 *Venir:*   ....

Practice (2): Making informal commands and requests with reflexive verbs

Using the **tú** form, change the following reflexive verbs into the Informal Imperative. Do not forget to place an accent where appropriate.

1 *¡(Acostarse) en seguida!*

2 *¡(Lavarse) las manos!*

3 *(Ponerse) la chaqueta gruesa.*

4 *(Quitarse) las botas.*

5 *¡(Callarse)!*

6 *¡No (enfadarse)!*

7 *¡No (irse)! (Quedarse) un rato.*

8 *¡No (burlarse) de mí!*

9 *¡No (moverse)!*

10 *¡No (hacerse) el tonto!*

Practice (3): Telling someone not to do something (using verb + pronoun)

Change the following from positive to negative.

eg *Tócalo.* = *No lo toques.*

1 *Ponlo aquí.* =
2 *Hazlo ahora.* =
3 *Cómelo.* =
4 *Acércate.* =
5 *Háblame así.* =
6 *Empújame.* =
7 *Espérame.* =
8 *Siéntate allí.* =

Practice (4): Giving instructions

In the following extract, José explains to Lola (who has now recovered) how to perform the card trick he showed her.

Change each verb in brackets into the Informal Imperative, adding a pronoun where indicated.

Primero (dejar) que un amigo tuyo escoja una carta de la baraja. (Pedir + le) que recuerde de qué carta se trata, pero que no te la enseñe. Mientras tu amigo mira su carta, (observar) rápidamente cuál es la que ha quedado debajo de la baraja. Pero (hacer + lo) muy de prisa para que él no te vea observando la última carta.

Ahora, (decir + le) al amigo que ponga su carta encima de las otras. (Tomar) la última carta de la baraja y (colocar + la) encima. Entonces (barajar) los naipes tantas veces como quieras, pero (hacer + lo) de tal modo que las dos cartas superiores no cambien de posición en la baraja.

A continuación, (dividir) la baraja en dos grupos y (colocar) encima la parte que estaba debajo. Luego, (extender) la baraja y (examinar) las cartas una a una hasta encontrar la escogida por tu amigo. Sabrás cuál es porque vendrá a continuación de la que tú observaste.

Extra reference

Note the following expression:

¡Estáte quieto! = Keep still! / Behave yourself! (In this particular case, **estar** acts as a reflexive verb.)

7.2 Forming and using the Future tense.

te hará bien   aguantaré   viajaremos   te enseñaré   sacaré

● Forming the Future tense

The Future tense is formed by adding the endings **-é, ás, -á, -emos, -éis, -án** to the full infinitive.

Hablar	Volver	Sentir
hablaré	*volveré*	*sentiré*
hablarás	*volverás*	*sentirás*
hablará	*volverá*	*sentirá*
hablaremos	*volveremos*	*sentiremos*
hablaréis	*volveréis*	*sentiréis*
hablarán	*volverán*	*sentirán*

Note that all the endings carry an accent, except **-emos**.

● **Irregular verbs**

The following verbs are irregular in the future and should be learnt by heart:

caber – cabré (-ás, -á..etc)	*saber – sabré*
decir – diré	*salir – saldré*
haber – habré	*tener – tendré*
poder – podré	*valer – valdré*
querer – querré	*venir – vendré*

● **Using the Future tense**

As in English, the Future tense in Spanish describes an action that has yet to take place.

Cumplirá 61 años en febrero. = He will be 61 years old in February.

Siempre recordaré aquel día. = I will always remember that day.

● **Using the Present tense in Spanish to express a future idea**

Do not forget that in spoken Spanish the Present tense is often used to refer to the immediate future.

¿Qué hago? = What shall I do?

Te veo mañana. = I'll see you tomorrow.

● **Using ir + a + verb to refer to the future**

Another way of stating the future is to use the present tense of **ir** + **a** + Infinitive.

Creo que me voy a desmayar. = I think I'm going to faint.

Te voy a enseñar un truco. = I'm going to show you a trick.

● **Using pronouns with the Future tense**

When a verb is in the future form, any pronoun is placed in front of it.

Te llamaré mañana. = I'll call you tomorrow.

Practice (5): Predicting the future

Look at the following extracts from a horoscope. Using the **tú** form, change each verb in brackets into the Future tense.

ARIES (21 marzo – 20 abril)

(Estar) más activo que de costumbre y (tomar) más iniciativas de lo normal: (sorprender) mucho. Días de mucho movimiento y mucha vida social en los que (renovar) tu círculo amistoso.

TAURO (21 abril – 20 mayo)

(Poder) realizar con facilidad actividades vocacionales que te habían resultado difíciles antes. (Empezar) a tener más en cuenta tu forma física y (cambiar) algunas de tus costumbres para sentirte mejor. (Hacer) más ejercicio y (liberar) tensiones.

VIRGO (24 agosto – 23 septiembre)

(Tener) dificultades en tu vida sentimental. Pero no hay duda de que (salir) de estas dificultades con un reforzamiento de tu personalidad.

LIBRA (24 septiembre – 23 octubre)

Días tranquilos en los que (conocer) a una persona interesante y (descubrir) nuevos lugares para pasar el tiempo libre.

CAPRICORNIO (21 diciembre – 20 enero)

(Empezar) a poder tener más tiempo para ti mismo y a la vez (sentirse) más romántico que de costumbre.

Practice (6): Expressing future possibility

Match items 1–5 with items a–e, changing each verb in brackets into
either the Present tense (after **si**) or the Future tense.

1 *Si yo lo (encontrar),*
2 *Si ella (tomar) esta medicina,*
3 *Yo te (perdonar) si me (prometer)*
4 *Si usted (seguir) con sus amenazas,*
5 *Si algún día (tener) suficiente dinero,*

a *(sentirse) mejor.*
b *(llamar) a la policía.*
c *yo (comprar) una casita en el campo.*
d *que nunca (volver) a hacerlo.*
e *te lo (dar).*

Practice (7): Using the Future tense instead of **ir + a**

Using the Future tense, rewrite the following sentences.

eg *Voy a verla mañana.*
    La veré mañana.

1 *Vamos a visitarles pasado mañana.*
   ....

2 *Van a hacerlo esta tarde.*
   ....

3 *Estoy seguro de que Juan va a ayudarnos.*
   ....

4 *Tu padre va a contarte una historia.*
   ....

5 *Han prometido que van a terminarlo pronto.*
   ....

Extra reference

✦ Using the future tense in Spanish to express assumption

The future tense in Spanish has one particular function that should be noted very carefully. Used in a statement, it can express an assumption based on a degree of certainty. Used in a question, it can express uncertainty.

This particular usage can cause a lot of confusion when translating from Spanish into English, so study very carefully the examples below. Note how succint the usage is in Spanish, and how varied the translations can be in English.

Tendrá unos treinta años. = He's about thirty. (*approximation*)
He must be about thirty. (*assumption*)
He's probably around thirty. (*probability*).

No ha comido en todo el día. Tendrá hambre.
He hasn't eaten all day. He must be hungry. / I'm sure he is hungry. / I suppose he is hungry.

Alguien llama a la puerta. ¿Quién será?
There's someone at the door. Who can it be? / I wonder who it is. / Who do you suppose it is?

¿Dónde estarán? = Where can they be?

✦ The problem of translating such phrases as *Will you take a seat, please?* into Spanish

There is a further aspect of the future tense that can also lead to confusion in translation; but this time from English into Spanish.

In English a polite or emphatic request can be expressed by the future tense, but not so in Spanish. Either use the Imperative form or use **querer** + Infinitive.

Will you sign here please? = *¿Quiere firmar aquí? (Firme aquí, por favor.)*

Will you shut up? = *¿Quiere callarse? (¡Cállese!)*

7.3 Using the Future tense in conjunction with the Present Subjunctive

aguantaré hasta que lleguemos   cuando vuelvas te voy a enseñar...

● **Using the Present Subjunctive after such words as cuando (when) and mientras (while, as long as)**

The Future tense (both in Spanish and in English) is often used in conjunction with another phrase. The problem is that in English we use the Present tense in conjunction with the Future tense, whereas in Spanish (except when we use **si** meaning **if**) the Present Subjunctive is used in conjunction with the Future tense. Look carefully at the following example:

I'll do it when I get back. = *Yo lo haré cuando vuelva.*

Of all the usages of the Present Subjunctive, this is the one that initially causes most problems for English speakers. This does not mean to say that this usage is difficult; merely that it is radically different from English usage and therefore requires careful attention.

● **What exactly is a conjunction?**

The following words are conjunctions (that is to say, they act as linking words):

cuando (when); *hasta que* (until); *en cuanto* (as soon as); *mientras* (while, as long as).

In Spanish when these conjunctions are used with statements that refer to the future (however vaguely), the Present Subjunctive must be used.

Esperaremos aquí hasta que vuelva.
We'll wait here until he comes back.
(*he hasn't come back – so it is not a definite fact.*)

Saldremos cuando deje de llover.
We'll go out when it stops raining.
(*it hasn't stopped raining – so the time referred to is indefinite.*)

...y te querré mientras viva.
...and I'll love you for as long as I live.
(I don't know how long I will live – so the time framework is indefinite.)

● **An exception to the rule: si (if).**

As you have already seen, **si** (which also is a conjunction) does not take the Present Subjunctive when used in sentences expressing future possibility.

Si te comportas bien, te compraré un regalo.
If you behave yourself, I'll buy you a present.

Si apruebas el examen, te daré cien libras.
If you pass the exam, I'll give you a hundred pounds.

● **Using the Present Indicative after conjunctions**

It is equally important not to forget, when learning the above, that the very same conjunctions just mentioned (**cuando/hasta que/en cuanto/mientras**) will be followed by a phrase in the Present tense (Indicative) if the phrase is not dependent on a future clause and refers to a definite fact in the present.

Me gusta trabajar en el jardín cuando tengo tiempo.
I like to work in the garden when I have time.

No me gusta salir cuando hace frío.
I don't like to go out when it is cold.

Practice (8): Using the Present Subjunctive in conjunction with the Future tense

Change each verb in brackets into either the Future tense or the Present Subjunctive.

1   *No sé cómo (reaccionar) mi marido cuando (enterarse) de este asunto.*
2   *No te preocupes. Tu hijo (aprender) a leer cuando (ir) a la escuela.*
3   *Yo te (mandar) una postal cuando (llegar) a Madrid.*
4   *Yo (seguir) trabajando mientras Dios me (dar) salud.*
5   *Aunque ella tiene setenta años, dice que (seguir) enseñando mientras (poder).*

Practice (9): Recognising when to use the Present Subjunctive or Indicative after certain conjunctions

Change each verb in brackets into the correct form of the Present tense (Indicative) or the Present Subjunctive.

1 *Siempre lo paso bien cuando (ir) a Francia.*

2 *Te voy a echar de menos cuando tú (ir) a Francia.*

3 *Yo lo haré cuando (tener) tiempo.*

4 *Cuando (estar) de buen humor, Pilar es una compañera divertida.*

5 *Voy a comprar un coche cuando (tener) dieciocho años.*

6 *Voy a buscar otro empleo cuando (regresar) de España.*

7 *Te devolveré el dinero en cuanto (poder).*

8 *En cuanto (llegar) la primavera, me siento feliz.*

9 *Voy a tomar unas vacaciones cuando (salir) del hospital.*

10 *Mi marido siempre se pone de mal humor cuando nosotros (tener) visita.*

11 *Mientras tu madre (seguir) en esa condición, no podremos operar.*

12 *Generalmente escucho la radio mientras (hacer) los deberes.*

Extra reference

✦ The Present Perfect Subjunctive

The Present Perfect Subjunctive may also follow a conjunction when referring to the future.

No lo toques hasta que se haya enfriado.
Don't touch it until it has cooled down.

(The Present Perfect Subjunctive is formed by the Present Subjunctive of **haber** + Past Participle.)

✦ Developing vocabulary: other conjunctions

There are other conjunctions that also may be followed by either the Subjunctive or the Indicative, depending on the precise mood of the verb.

The most important of these are as follows:

tan pronto como = as soon as

siempre que = whenever/as long as/provided

de manera que / de modo que = so that (When **so that** implies *aim/purpose* it takes the subjunctive; when it indicates *result*, it takes the indicative.)

aunque   = although/even if

a pesar de que   = despite the fact

después (de) que = after

como   = as (When **as** means *since/because*, it is always followed by the Indicative.)

Look carefully at the following examples:

Lo haré tan pronto como pueda.
I'll do it as soon as I can. (subj.)

Jugaremos al tenis mañana siempre que no llueva.
We'll play tennis tomorrow as long as it doesn't rain. (subj.)

Siempre que salimos, discutimos.
Whenever we go out, we argue. (indic.)

Aunque haga mal tiempo, iremos a la playa.
Even if the weather is bad, we will go to the beach. (subj.)

Aunque es rico, es infeliz.
Although he's rich, he's unhappy. (indic.)

Debes colocar la planta de modo que reciba suficiente luz.
You must position the plant so that it gets enough light. (subj.)

Trata de hacerlo de tal manera que nadie te vea.
Try and do it in such a way that nobody sees you. (subj.)

Hazlo tantas veces como quieras.
Do it as many times as you like. (subj.)

Como no tengo nada que hacer, voy a acostarme.
As I've got nothing to do, I'm going to bed. (indic.)

7.4 Conjunctions that are always followed by the subjunctive.

para que te distraigas

● Not all conjunctions are as complicated as the ones listed in 7.3. The following conjunctions, for example, are always followed by the subjunctive:

para que/a fin de que	= in order that/so that
a condición de que	= on condition that
con tal que	= provided that/as long as
a menos que/a no ser que	= unless
antes (de) que	= before
como si	= as if (Only used with the past subjunctive.)
sin que	= without
en caso de que	= in case

NB: If there is no change of subject, the Infinitive is used after **para, antes de** and **sin**.

Se fue sin decirme nada. = He went off without saying anything to me.

Practice (10): Becoming familiar with conjunctions + the Present Subjunctive

Match items 1–10 with items a–j changing each verb in brackets into the correct form of the Present Subjunctive.

1 *Te voy a dar cinco mil pesetas*
2 *Abre un poco la ventana*
3 *Ponlo a fuego lento*
4 *Generalmente no tomo vino*
5 *No llegarás a tiempo*
6 *Puedes usar la moto*
7 *Te prestaré el libro*
8 *¿Puedes hacerlo*
9 *Quiero terminar*
10 *Lleva este paraguas*

a   *para que (salir) el olor.*
b   *a menos que (marcharse) ahora mismo.*
c   *a condición de que la (cuidar) bien.*
d   *sin que Pedro (enterarse)?*
e   *en caso de que (llover).*
f   *antes de que ellos (llegar).*
g   *para que no (quemarse).*
h   *para que (comprar) unos zapatos nuevos.*
i   *a menos que (ser) una ocasión especial.*
j   *con tal que me lo (devolver) pronto.*

Extra reference

✦ Por mucho que

Another subjunctive construction you need to recognise is **por** (+ adjective/adverb) + **que** + Subjunctive (However/No matter how...).

...por mucho que dure el viaje.
...however long the journey might take.

No podrás levantar este peso, por (muy) fuerte que seas.
You won't be able to lift this weight, however strong you are/might be.

Por mucho dinero que me ofrezcan, no venderé este cuadro.
No matter how much money I am offered, I shall not sell this painting.

NB: It is possible to use the Indicative after this construction (usually when the verb is in the past):

Por más que les rogaba, no me dejaban hacerlo.
However much I pleaded with them, they wouldn't let me do it.

Por mucho que se esforzaba, no lograba repararlo.
However hard he tried, he couldn't manage to repair it.

Por mucho que trataron, no pudieron convencerle.
However hard they tried, they couldn't convince him.

7.5 Indicating a change of state.

¡Te has puesto muy pálida!

- **Indicating a change of state in English**

  In English we use such verbs as **become, get, go, turn** and **grow** to indicate a change of state:

  He became ill.   She got angry.   He went red.   It turned green.   He grew tired.

- **Making a verb reflexive to indicate a change of state**

  In Spanish a change of state can usually be shown by making an appropriate verb reflexive:

  enfadarse (to become angry); *cansarse* (to grow tired); *aburrirse* (to get bored).

  Sometimes it is not even necessary to make a verb reflexive:

  adelgazar (to become thin); *engordar* (to become fat); *envejecer* (to grow old).

- **Ponerse, volverse, hacerse, convertirse en,**

  Alternatively, one can use **ponerse/volverse/hacerse/convertirse en** + the appropriate state/condition. Note carefully how the different verbs are used:

  i) **Ponerse**

  This verb is used primarily for emotional states, and for changes in physical condition and/or appearance. Usually **ponerse** expresses a temporary condition.

Se puso rojo.	= He went red.
Se puso muy triste.	= He became very sad.
Se está poniendo frío.	= It's getting cold.
¡Te estás poniendo gordo!	= You're getting fat!

ii) **Volverse**

This verb expresses a more permanent condition than **ponerse** and is used mainly for changes in character/nature.

Se ha vuelto loco.	= He's gone mad.
Se ha vuelto muy arrogante.	= He has become very arrogant.
Se ha vuelto negro.	= It has turned black.

iii) **Hacerse**

Hacerse is mainly used to show the result of some kind of effort or voluntary decision.

Se hizo monja.	= She became a nun.
Se hizo rico.	= He became rich.

As we have already seen, there are also many idiomatic expressions with hacerse.

Se está haciendo tarde.	= It's getting late.

iv) **Convertirse en**

This verb is used with nouns or noun phrases and shows a complete transformation.

Se ha convertido en un actor muy famoso.
He has become a very famous actor.

Se ha convertido en mi peor enemigo.
He has become my worst enemy.

Practice (11): Indicating a change of state

Of the four alternatives, which one(s) can go with the verb given? More than one alternative may be correct.

1) *Se puso ... .*

    a *contento*

    b *furioso*

    c *mi mejor amigo.*

    d *nervioso*

2) *Se ha vuelto ... .*

    a *triste*

    b *muy vago*

    c *tacaño*

    d *muy desconfiado*

3) *Se hizo ... .*

    a *loco*

    b *abogado*

    c *gordo*

    d *sucio*

4) *Se ha convertido en ... .*

    a *un niño muy travieso*

    b *orgulloso*

    c *serio*

    d *un buen trabajador*

Extra reference

✦ Other ways of translating **become**

- When **become** contains the idea of having lost something, then **quedarse** may be used:

    Se quedó ciega. = She became blind.

- When **become** contains the idea of a long-term achievement, **llegar a ser** is used.

    Llegó a ser presidente de la compañía.
    He (*eventually*) became president of the company.

(**Llegar a** + Infinitive means **to manage to do something**.)

7.6 Placing object pronouns in correct order.

No me la enseñes

- **The usual order of pronouns**

  When two object pronouns appear together, the order in which one pronoun follows another is as follows:

1	2	3	4
se	te, os	me, nos	le, les, lo, los, la, las

Enséñamelas.	= Show them to me.
Dámelo.	= Give it to me.
Mañana te lo explico todo.	= Tomorrow I'll tell you all about it.
¡Se me ha caído el florero!	= I've dropped the vase!

  Lo primero que se le ocurrió a Pedro fue...
  The first thing that occurred to Pedro was to...

- **Replacing le/les with se**

  In theory, **le/les** (indirect) should precede **lo/los/la/las** (direct), but in fact this never happens. The rule is that **le** or **les** becomes **se** when followed by **lo/los/la/las**.

  Se lo daré mañana. = I'll give it to him/her/you/them tomorrow.

  You can make it clear who you are referring to by positioning **a** + pronoun after the statement.

  Se lo daré a él/ellos.
  Se lo daré a ella/ellas.
  Se lo daré a usted/ustedes.

Practice (12): Placing object pronouns in correct position

Rewrite the sentences below, placing the words in correct order.

1 *¿lo quién mandó te?*
2 *¿prestas me la?*
3 *¿que muestre quieres lo te?*
4 *ofrecieron él a lo se.*
5 *¡ella a no los se enseñes!*

Progress test 7

Translate the following into Spanish. Wherever you need to use an Imperative, use the **tú** form of the Informal Imperative.

1 I will do it later if I have time.

2 He says he will do it when he has time.

3 If we arrive before eight o'clock, we will be able to catch the fast train.

4 We will call you as soon as we arrive.

5 We will wait here until it stops raining.

6 I am going to give you a map so that you don't get lost. (Use *perderse*)

7 Call her now so that she knows you are all right.

8 Don't call me unless it is really urgent.

9 Provided that the train leaves on time, I'll be there at eight.

10 I usually leave very early, before the others get up.

11 Don't touch that machine!

12 He went red when she told him she loved him.

13 He became rich and famous.

14 She has become arrogant and lazy.

15 It is his book. Give it to him!

UNIT 8 Making comparisons and expressing emotions

Rosa arrives home after an evening out. She is greeted by her mother.

Madre: ¿Qué tal la película?

Rosa: Bien, mamá.

Madre: Pareces un poco agitada. ¿Te pasa algo?

Rosa: Escucha, mamá. Quiero decirte algo, pero <u>estoy tan nerviosa que apenas puedo hablar.</u>   8.2 8.4

Madre: ¿Nerviosa? Pero, ¿por qué?

Rosa: <u>Será mejor que te sientes</u> antes que te cuente lo que ha pasado.   8.7

Madre: ¿Qué ha ocurrido? Dime.

Rosa: Siéntate mamá, por favor.

Madre: ¡Cuéntame, por Dios! ¿Qué ha sucedido?

Rosa: ¿Te acuerdas de Carlos, mamá?

Madre: Claro que me acuerdo de él. <u>Espero que no me vayas a decir</u> que habéis vuelto a ser novios. <u>Nos dijiste que habías acabado con él.</u> Sabes muy bien que tu padre se opone a que salgas con ese hombre. Y hablando de tu padre, <u>me extraña que no haya venido</u> a cenar. ¿Dónde estará?   8.7 8.1 8.7

Rosa: Escúchame, mamá. Me ha pedido la mano.

Madre: ¿La mano? ¿Qué mano? ¡Santo Dios! He oído lo que has dicho, pero no lo creo.

Rosa: Le he dicho que sí, mamá. Voy a casarme con Carlos.

Madre: ¡¡¿Casarte?!! ¡¿Con Carlos?! ¡No puede ser! ¿Te has vuelto loca o qué? <u>Tu padre no te va a permitir que</u>   8.5
<u>te cases con él.</u> <u>Y yo tampoco.</u> Rosa, quiero saber   8.4
una cosa. Dime la verdad. ¿Estás embarazada?

Rosa: No, mamá.

Madre: ¡Qué alivio! <u>Bendito sea Dios.</u> Ahora escúchame   8.7
bien, Rosa. Tú no tienes más que diecisiete años.
Eres demasiado joven para casarte. Aún eres una
niña. En cambio, Carlos tiene treinta y cinco años.
<u>Es mucho mayor que tú.</u>   8.3

Rosa: Pero <u>tú eres más joven que papá.</u>   8.3

Madre: Sí, pero tu padre es un hombre bueno y honrado;
Carlos no lo es.

Rosa: <u>¡Carlos no es tan malo como cree todo el mundo!</u>   8.2

Madre: <u>No digo que sea malo,</u> pero es un hombre   8.6
divorciado y tiene un hijo de cinco años. ¿Qué van a
pensar los vecinos?

Rosa: <u>¡Que piensen lo que quieran!</u>   8.7/8.8

Madre: Mira, Rosa, ¿por qué no esperamos a que vuelva tu
padre y entonces seguiremos hablando?

Rosa: Bueno, pero pase lo que pase me voy a casar con
Carlos.

Madre: ¡Ay, hija mía! tu padre se va a poner como una fiera
cuando oiga esta noticia!… Ah, mira, aquí está.
Pero, ¿quién está con él?

Rosa: Es su secretaria, la rubia.

Padre: Hola, querida. Hola, Rosita. Conocéis a Teresa,
¿verdad? Pues… ¿Queréis sentaros un momento?
Es que tengo algo importante que deciros, pero
estoy tan nervioso que apenas puedo hablar.

8.1 Forming and using the Past Perfect

Nos dijiste que habías acabado con él.

● **What is the Past Perfect (or Pluperfect) tense?**

In general terms, the Past Perfect (or Pluperfect) tense in Spanish corresponds to the Past Perfect in English.

Había nevado durante la noche.
It had snowed during the night.

Aquel día ella se había levantado temprano.
That day she had got up early.

● **Forming the Past Perfect**

The Past Perfect is formed by the Imperfect of **haber + Past Participle**.

(yo)	*había visto*	– I had seen
(tú)	*habías olvidado*	– you had forgotten
(él, ella, Vd)	*había pensado*	– he/she/you had thought
(nosotros/as)	*habíamos creído*	– we had believed
(vosotros/as)	*habíais sabido*	– you had known
(ellos/as, Vds)	*habían comido*	– they/you had eaten

● **Using the Imperfect instead of the Past Perfect tense in certain time constructions**

As we have already seen, certain time constructions need to be learnt separately (See 5.1, the Imperfect tense).

No la reconocí inmediatamente porque llevaba más de quince años sin verla.
I didn't recognise her immediately because I hadn't seen her for more than fifteen years.

Hacía tres meses que trabajaba en Perú cuando descubrí que...
I had been working in Peru for three months when I discovered that...

● **Using the correct tense with acabar**

Be careful with **acabar**. When it takes its literal meaning of **to finish/end**, **acabar** follows the normal patterns of tense formation.

Nos dijiste que habías acabado con él.
You told us that you had finished with him / that it was all over between you and him.

Acabaron por despedirla. = They ended up sacking her.

However, **acabar** + **de** + Infinitive is a special time construction.

Acaba de salir. = He has just gone out.

Acababa de salir. = He had just gone out.

Practice (1): Using the Past Perfect tense in context

Select an appropriate verb for each of the gaps below, and then change it into the correct form of the Past Perfect.

robar comer viajar marcharse dormir oír esconder tener gastar pasar.

1 *Cuando llegamos, descubrimos que los otros ya ....*

2 *Cuando se dio cuenta de que le .... , Pedro llamó a la policía.*

3 *Volvieron al hotel en el cual .... su luna de miel.*

4 *Cuando llegué a casa, tenía mucha hambre porque no .... en todo el día.*

5 *Mi hermano estaba muy cansado porque no .... bien la noche anterior.*

6 *Estaba nerviosa cuando subió a bordo porque nunca .... en avión.*

7 *Estando seguro de que .... un ruido extraño, bajé las escaleras con un bastón en la mano.*

8 *Encontraron la caja en la cual los ladrones .... el dinero.*

9 *Mi madre se puso furiosa cuando le expliqué que yo .... todo el dinero.*

10 *Llegó tarde porque .... un accidente.*

Extra reference

✦ Recognising the Past Anterior tense (literary Spanish)

There is a special literary tense called the Past Anterior (or Preterite Perfect) which is used instead of the Past Perfect in specific time phrases. This is not something that you should particularly worry about, since it is rarely used in speech and can be easily avoided in your own writing.

The Past Anterior is formed by the preterite of **haber (hube, hubiste, hubo, hubimos, hubisteis, hubieron)** + Past Participle.

This tense is found after such conjunctions as **cuando/apenas/en cuanto/tan pronto como/hasta que,** and is always used in conjunction with a verb in the preterite.

Apenas hubo cerrado la puerta cuando sonó el teléfono.
No sooner had he shut the door than the telephone rang.
(*Hardly/Scarcely had...when...*)

En cuanto hubo terminado el trabajo, se fue para la casa.
As soon as he had finished the work, he went off home.

No hizo nada hasta que todos se hubieron marchado.
He did nothing until they had all left.

✦ Avoiding the Past Anterior
NB:
a) You can avoid this tense by simply using the preterite.

Apenas me vio, se echó a reír.
As soon as he saw me, he started laughing.

En cuanto terminó el trabajo, se fue a casa.
As soon as he finished the work, he went off home.

b) The Past Anterior can also be avoided by using a past participle clause (Past Participle + object).

Terminado el trabajo, se fue a ver a sus amigos.
The work (being) finished, he went off to see his friends.

c) The following is a useful phrase to learn:

Dicho y hecho. = No sooner said than done.

8.2 Distinguishing between **tan...que** and **tan...como.**

..estoy tan nerviosa que apenas puedo hablar. ¡Carlos no es tan malo como cree todo el mundo!

● Linking tan with tanto

In learning to distinguish between **tan...que** and **tan...como**, you should also learn to distinguish between **tanto...que** and **tanto...como**. After both **tan** and **tanto**, **que** means **that** (showing consequence) and **como** means **as** (in a comparison of equality or similarity). Now study very carefully the following examples of **tan/tanto** with **que/como**.

- ● **Understanding how to use tan** (+ adjective/adverb)

  i) **tan...que** = so...that

  Es tan difícil que nadie puede hacerlo.
  It's so difficult that nobody can do it.

  Habla tan de prisa que nadie le entiende.
  He speaks so fast that nobody understands him.

  ii) **tan...como** = as...as / so...as

  Pedro no es tan simpático como José.
  Pedro is not as nice as José.

  No es tan maravilloso como todos creen.
  It's not so marvellous as everybody thinks.

  No es tan difícil como parece.
  It's not as difficult as it looks.

- ● **Using tanto** (with verb / + noun)

  i) **tanto...que** = so much...that / so...that

  Hace tanto calor que no tengo ganas de hacer nada.
  It's so hot that I don't feel like doing anything.

  Comió tanto que se puso enfermo.
  He ate so much that he fell ill.

  Me asusté tanto que casi me desmayé.
  I was so shocked that I almost fainted.

  (Note that in front of a noun, **tanto** acts as a normal adjective:
  Tenía tanta hambre que comió cinco huevos.
  He was so hungry that he ate five eggs.)

  ii) **tanto...como** = as much...as

  No gano tanto como tú.
  I don't earn as much as you (do).

  Again note that **tanto** acts as a normal adjective in front of a noun:

  Hay tantos niños como niñas en la clase.
  There are as many boys as girls in the class.

● **Using que not como in a comparison of equality or similarity**

NB: When used with **tan/tanto, que** means **that**. When used with **igual/lo mismo, que** means **as**.

Haré exactamente lo mismo que ellos.
I shall do exactly the same as them.

Se bebe mucho vino en Francia, igual que en España.
They drink a lot of wine in France, the same as in Spain.

Practice (2): Distinguishing between **que** and **como**

Complete each gap with either **que** or **como**.

1 *Bebió tanto .... se puso enfermo.*

2 *Para llegar a la cumbre de la montaña más alta del mundo, es necesario subir tan alto .... los aviones en su vuelo. Esta altísima montaña es el Everest.*

3 *Hace más de dos mil años, los romanos crearon un extenso imperio y una gran cultura, tan importante .... de ella deriva gran parte de la cultura occidental de hoy.*

4 *En Egipto hay una estatua tan grande .... en cada uno de sus pies pueden sentarse ocho personas. Es una de las gigantescas estatuas del rey Ramsés.*

5 *Ella tiene los cabellos tan finos .... la seda más fina.*

6 *Hay mendigos por las calles de Bogotá, igual .... en Londres.*

7 *Andrés no es tan inteligente .... su hermano.*

8 *Poca gente ha sufrido tanto .... ella.*

9 *Trataré de estar allí tan pronto .... posible.*

10 *¡La luna brilla tanto .... parece de día! —exclamó Marta.*

Extra reference

✦ Omitting **tan** in a comparison of equality

In a comparison of equality ("as...as"), **tan** can be omitted.

Ella tiene la piel blanca como la nieve.
Her skin is as white as snow.

✦ A special use of **tanto...como**

Note carefully the idiomatic use of **tanto...como** as a way of emphasising the idea of *both* rather than one or the other:

Tanto María como Ana tienen la culpa.
Both María and Ana are to blame.

Nadie es perfecto. Tanto los ingleses como los españoles tienen sus defectos.
Nobody is perfect. Both the English and the Spanish have their faults.

NB: Note that in the examples above, **tanto** is neutral and does not agree with the noun that follows.

8.3 Forming comparatives and superlatives.

Es mucho mayor que tú. Tú eres más joven que papá.

● General observation:

Forming comparatives (eg better, bigger) and superlatives (eg the best, the biggest) is fairly straightforward in Spanish, once you are aware of certain problem areas.

Do not forget that comparisons of equality (**tan/tanto...como; igual/lo mismo que**) are dealt with in 8.2, and that the difference between **más que** and **más de** is discussed in 5.5.

- ● **The comparative form**

    i) Making comparisons with adjectives

a) Using **más...que** and **menos...que**

  With most adjectives, a comparison is made by using
  más...que or **menos...que**.

  Antonio es más alto y flaco que su hermano.
  Antonio is taller and thinner than his brother.

  Este libro es menos interesante que el otro.
  This book is less interesting than the other one.

b) Using **mejor** and **peor**

  The comparative form of **bueno** is **mejor** (better), and the
  comparative form of **malo** is **peor** (worse).

  Creo que esta máquina es mejor que ésa.
  I think this machine is better than that one.

  La otra profesora era mala, pero la nueva es peor.
  The other teacher was bad, but the new one is worse.

c) Using **más grande** or **mayor**

  The comparative form of **grande** is either **más grande** or
  mayor.

  – **Más grande** refers to physical size only.

Francia es más grande que Italia.
France is larger than Italy.

Antonio es más grande que Manuel.
Antonio is bigger than Manuel.

– **Mayor** can also refer to physical size (things or animals).

La mayoría de los calamares (squid) no son mayores que la mano del hombre. Pero los calamares gigantes son más largos que dos autobuses puestos en fila.

NB: Note that **largo** means **long** – not *large*:

El cuello de la jirafa es más largo que todo su cuerpo.
The giraffe's neck is longer than the whole of its body.

– With people, **mayor** refers to age.

Ella es mayor que María.
She is older than María.

Tengo una hermana mayor.
I have an older sister.

d) Using **menor, más jóven** and **más pequeño**

The opposite of **mayor** is **menor**. However, be very careful. When used with people, it is placed after the person concerned.

Tengo un hermano menor.
I have a younger brother.

– When comparing ages, use **más jóven que**. Do not use **menor**.

Ella es más jóven que Rosa
She is younger than Rosa.

– When comparing size, use **más pequeño que**. Do not use **menor**.

Aunque tiene la misma edad, este bebé es más pequeño que ése.
Although they are the same age, this baby is smaller than that one.

e) Using **menos**

The comparative form of **poco(s)** is **menos**.

Hay menos estudiantes en la clase este año
There are fewer students in the class this year.

ii) Making comparisons with adverbs

a) The similarity of form with adjectives

With adverbs, a comparison is also made by using **más...que** or **menos...que**. The only irregular adverbs are:

bien – *mejor*
mal – *peor*
mucho – *más*
poco – *menos*

(Note that **mejor/peor/más/menos** function both as adjectives and adverbs.)

¡Hombre tú conduces más despacio que tu abuela.
You drive more slowly than your grandmother!

Andrés toca la guitarra mejor que Paco.
Andrés plays the guitar better than Paco.

b) Translating the adverbial phrase, **more than ever**.

Note that **more than ever** is translated as **más que nunca**.

Le quiero más que nunca. = I love him more than ever.

c) Study very carefully the following examples of dependent comparatives.

Cuanto antes, mejor. = The sooner, the better.

Cuanto más, mejor. = The more, the better.

Cuanto más le doy, más quiere. = The more I give him, the more he wants.

It is possible to put **tanto** in the second half of this structure.

Cuanto más gano, tanto más gasto.
The more I earn, the more I spend.

● The superlative form

i) **Adjectives**

a) To make an adjective into a superlative, simply add the definite article (**el/la/los/las**) to the comparative form of the adjective. If the preceding noun already has the definite article, merely add the comparative form of the adjective.

Manuel es el más alto de la clase.
Manuel is the tallest in the class.

El niño más alto de la clase es Manuel.
The tallest boy in the class is Manuel.

NB: Out of context, **el niño más alto** can be either comparative or superlative: the **taller** boy or **the tallest** boy.

b) If **in** follows a superlative phrase, it is translated by **de**.

Istanbul es la mayor ciudad de Turquía y una de las más antiguas del mundo.
Istanbul is the largest city in Turkey and one of the most ancient in the world.

c) Note, however, that **in** is translated as **en** when a comparative phrase is used. Compare the following examples. They mean the same, but they are structurally different.

No hay mejor restaurante en Londres.
There's no better restaurant in London.

Es el mejor restaurante de Londres.
It is the best restaurant in London.

d) Note very carefully the following meanings of **mayor** and **menor** when used with the definite article.

—*Tengo tres hijos: el mayor tiene doce años y el menor seis años.*
I have got three sons: the oldest/eldest is twelve and the youngest six.

—*La hija mayor se llama Rosa y la hija menor se llama Consuelo.*
The eldest daughter is called Rosa and the youngest daughter is called Consuelo.

—*El topo pasa la mayor parte de su vida bajo tierra.*
The mole spends the greatest part/most of its life under the ground.

—*La mayor parte de leones viven en Africa.*
Most/The majority of lions live in Africa.

More commonly, **the majority of/most** is translated as **la mayoría de**:

La mayoría de murciélagos comen insectos que cogen mientras vuelan.
Most bats eat insects which they catch while flying.

—*No tengo la menor idea.* = I don't have the slightest idea.

e) Note very carefully the use of **jamás** in a superlative phrase.

Es el mejor regalo que jamás he recibido.
It's the best present I have ever had.

It is also possible to use **nunca** in this type of construction, but it is less common. Occasionally you will find that the second part of this type of superlative statement is put in the Subjunctive (*...que jamás haya recibido*), but it is not obligatory to do so and is certainly not common in everyday speech.

ii) **Making superlative statements with adverbs**

The definite article is not used when forming the superlative of adverbs. The comparative form is used, and one relies on the context to determine whether the meaning is that of a comparative or a superlative.

¿Quién canta mejor? = Who sings better/best?

Practice (3): Forming comparative and superlative phrases

Write out the following sentences in full, extending the words given in brackets. In each case you will need to decide whether to use the comparative or superlative form, and to make any changes or additions accordingly.

eg *Groenlandia es (mayor isla) mundo.*
    = *Groenlandia es la mayor isla del mundo.*

1 *La Scala es (famoso teatro de ópera) Italia y uno de (famoso) mundo.*

2 *Dijo que era (mejor película) jamás había visto.*

3 *¡Hoy es (día feliz) mi vida!*

4 *La pitón reticulada es el reptil (largo). Es (largo) seis bicicletas puestas en fila.*

5 *Hace millones de años, los caballos no eran (mayor) los gatos.*

6 *Las pirañas viven en los ríos de América del Sur y son (peligroso) los tiburones.*

7 *El Empire State Building, de Nueva York, es uno (edificio alto) mundo.*

8 *Andorra es uno (país pequeño) mundo.*

9 *El guepardo es (rápido) los animales que corren.*

10 *Al oír la noticia, se sintió (feliz nunca).*

11 *Cuanto (le doy), (pide).*

12 *(la conozco), (la quiero).*

Extra reference

✦ The use of **...ísimo** as an alternative to a superlative phrase

There exists in Spanish what is known as the **Absolute Superlative** (adding the superlative suffix **...ísimo** to a word). When you feel, for example, that something is so good that there is no need to compare it with anything else you will naturally say *¡Es buenísimo!* – such a statement expresses utter contentment or approval. Look carefully at the following examples.

Es barato. Es baratísimo. = It's cheap. It's dirt cheap.

Es caro. Es carísimo. = It's expensive. It's far too expensive.

Es guapo. Es guapísimo. = He's good-looking. He's gorgeous.

✦ Translating **more and more**

Note the use of **cada vez más** (more and more):

...iba cada vez más de prisa
...it went faster and faster

se ponía cada vez más enojada
...she was getting angrier and angrier

✦ Translating **too / too much**

There are two things you need to remember when using **demasiado** (too/too much).

– Used as an adverb (after a verb or before an adjective), **demasiado** does not change its form; but in front of a noun it does.

El problema es que él trata de hacer demasiado con demasiada rapidez.
The problem is that he tries to do too much too quickly.

– When an infinitive follows **demasiado, para** should be used.

Eres demasiado joven para casarte.
You are too young to marry.

8.4 Using negative words

apenas puedo hablar **y yo tampoco**

● **Using negative words in English and Spanish**

When a negative word stands on its own or is the subject of a verb, there is no problem of usage: Spanish and English follow the same pattern.

—*¿Hay alguien allí?* —*No, nadie.* = *Is anybody there? No, nobody.*

Nadie sabe dónde está. = Nobody knows where he is.

However, in Spanish a negative word cannot stand on its own when it is the object of a verb. It must be accompanied by another negative word in front of the verb.

No hay nadie allí. = There is nobody there.

Nunca molesta a nadie. = He never bothers anybody.

NB: If **que** precedes a negative word, it is not necessary to put another negative word in front of the verb.

Dijo que no (He said no). *Supongo que no* (I suppose not).

● **A check-list of negative words in Spanish**

Look carefully at the following check-list of negative words, noting in particular the way they are translated in context.

1 No

Just like **¿verdad?**, **¿no?** can be used as a question tag.

Es cierto, ¿no? = It's true, isn't it?

– **Ya no** means **no longer**.

El dodó ya no existe. = The dodo no longer exists.

– **Todavía no** is the same as **aún no** (not yet/still not).

No han llegado todavía. = They haven't arrived yet.

Aún no han terminado. = They still haven't finished.

Be careful not to confuse **aún** (with accent, = still) with **aun** (no accent, = even).

2 Apenas

As a negative word, **apenas** has the basic meaning of **hardly**, meaning *almost not.*

Apenas puedo hablar = I can hardly speak (*Note the word order.*)

Apenas la conozco. = I hardly/barely/scarcely know her.

In literary Spanish you will sometimes come across **apenas si** instead of **apenas.**

3 Nada

Nada can mean **not at all** (in the same way that **algo** can mean **somewhat**: *algo sorprendido* = somewhat surprised).

No es nada fácil. = It's not at all easy. / It's not easy at all.

No me encuentro nada bien. = I don't feel at all well.

Note carefully the various other ways of translating **not at all**:

a) —*Gracias.*
—*De nada. / No hay de qué.* = Not at all (*You're welcome*).

b) —*No estorbo, ¿verdad?* = I'm not in the way, am I?
—*No, de ninguna manera.* = No, not at all.

c) —*¿Te molesta?* = Is it disturbing you?
—*No, en absoluto.* = No, not at all.

4 Nadie

Do not forget that the personal **a** is used with **nadie** when it is the object of a verb.

No conozco a nadie aquí. = I don't know anybody here.

Nadie más = Nobody else

5 Nunca/Jamás (See also 8.3)

These two words are usually interchangeable.

Jamás volveré. / Nunca volveré. = I will never go back.

The two words can be used together:

¡No vuelvas a hacer eso nunca jamás! = Don't ever do that again!

(More commonly, **nunca más** is used to translate **never again**.)

6 Ninguno

When acting as an adjective, **ninguno** becomes **ningún** in front of a singular masculine noun.

en ningún momento = at no point/at no time

When acting as a pronoun, **ninguno** usually means **none** (not one of many) or **neither** (of two things or people mentioned) and is, therefore, always found in the singular when used in this way.

—¿Cuáles de estos libros te gustan?
—Ninguno (de ellos). = None (of them).

—¿Cuál de estas dos camisas te gusta más?
—Ninguna. = Neither (of them).

7 Ni

Ni means **nor/neither**. Study carefully the following examples:

a) *Ni Pedro ni José fuma.* = Neither Pedro nor José smokes.

b) *Ni fuma ni bebe. / No fuma, ni bebe.*
He neither drinks nor smokes.

c) *No tengo ni vídeo ni televisión. / No tengo vídeo ni televisión.*
I have neither a video nor a television.

Ni can mean **not even**.

Ni me saludaron. = They didn't even say hello.

¡Ni se te ocurra! = Don't even think about it! / Don't you dare!

Ni can be reinforced with **siquiera** or **aun** to emphasise the idea of **not even**

Ni siquiera me miraron. = They didn't even look at me.

8 Tampoco

Tampoco is the negative form of **también**.

—Yo quiero ver la película.   —Yo también. (So do I.)

—Yo no quiero ver la película. —Yo tampoco. (Neither do I.)

Practice (4): Using **ninguno** in context

Complete the gaps below with the correct form of **ninguno**.

1 .... *reptil de los que hoy viven, serpiente, tortuga, lagarto, caimán, cocodrilo, puede volar. Pero hace ciento cincuenta millones de años había muchos reptiles voladores.*

2 *Las dos chicas hablan alemán, pero* .... *de las dos habla francés.*

3 *—¿Cuáles de estos discos te gustan?*
   —........ . Son todos malos.

4 *No veo* .... *manera de resolver el problema.*

5 *Esa frase no tiene* .... *sentido.*

6 *No soy miembro de* .... *partido político.*

Practice (5): Using **negative** words appropriately

Complete the gaps below with the following words:

siquiera nunca más jamás absoluto nadie ni...ni ni aún tampoco nada

1 *Esta noticia no me sorprende en* ....

2 .... *en aquella noche* .... *en la siguiente se presentó Martín.*

3 *Ni* .... *la miró una sola vez.*

4 *A* .... *se le permite tocar esta máquina.*

5 *—No tengo ganas de salir.*
　　—Yo .... *.*

6 *—¿Es urgente?*
　　—No, no es .... *importante.*

7 *—¿Te llevas bien con tus vecinos?*
　　—Hombre, ... *me saludan cuando me ven.*

8 *¡Qué hombre más ingrato. ¡* .... *le haré un favor!*

9 .... *no sabemos si está fuera de peligro.*

10 .... *olvidaré sus palabras. Siempre las recordaré.*

Extra reference

✦ A useful expression to learn is **no servir para nada.**

　Esta máquina no sirve para nada.
　This machine is useless.

　Todos mis esfuerzos no han servido para nada.
　All my efforts have been for nothing.

✦ In spoken Spanish you will often hear the exclamation, **¡Ni hablar!** (No fear! / Not likely! / No way! / Absolutely not! / Not on your life!).

　—¿Me prestas diez mil pesetas?
　Will you lend me 10,000 pesetas?

　—¡Ni hablar! Acúerdate que aún me debes cinco mil.
　No way! Remember you still owe me 5,000.

8.5 Verbs followed by either the Subjunctive or the Infinitive

Tu padre no te va a permitir que te cases con él

● **Using either the Subjunctive or Infinitive after certain verbs**

Just as the Subjunctive follows verbs of **wishing, wanting, telling** and **requesting** when there is a change of subject, so too the Subjunctive is to be found after other verbs which describe one person influencing the actions of another. Particular attention, however, should be paid to the following group of verbs since these verbs may be followed by *either* the Subjunctive or the Infinitive (irrespective of whether there is a change of subject).

● The most common verbs in this group are:

dejar/permitir	– to let/allow/permit
prohibir	– to forbid
impedir	– to prevent
mandar	– to order
aconsejar	– to advise

Although **hacer** also belongs to this group, it is best to use the Infinitive structure only.

Me hacen trabajar mucho. = They make me work a lot.

The verbs above must be followed by **que** if the Subjunctive is to be used.

● Now look carefully at the following examples:

a) *Deja que el papel se seque durante un día.*
Let the paper dry for a day.

Déjalo secar durante un día.
Let it dry for a day.

Deja que se seque durante un día.
Let it dry for a day.

b) *No me permiten salir/que salga sola por la noche.*
I am not allowed to go out on my own at night.

c) *Permiten a mi hermano salir/que salga solo por la noche.*
Permiten que mi hermano salga solo por la noche.
My brother is allowed to go out on his own at night.

d) *Me han prohibido salir/que salga con él.*
They have forbidden me to go out with him.

Practice (6): Recognising the dual sentence pattern that follows certain verbs

For each pair of sentences, finish off the second sentence so that it means exactly the same as the first.

1 *Calienta la leche, pero no dejes que hierva.*
Calienta la leche, pero no la dejes ....

2 *No lo comas todavía. Déjalo enfriar.*
No lo comas todavía. Deja que se ....

3 *Permítame ayudarle.*
Permítame que ....

4 *Permíteme decirte una cosa.*
Permíteme ....

5 *El médico me ha prohibido fumar.*
El médico me ha prohibido ....

6 *El médico no me permite comer carne.*
El médico no me permite ....

7 *Te prohíbo hablar con él.*
Te prohíbo ....

8 *Nos han aconsejado no viajar en coche por esa parte del país.*
Nos han aconsejado ....

9 *Te aconsejo estudiar otro idioma.*
Te aconsejo ....

10 *Te aconsejo buscar otro trabajo.*
Te aconsejo ....

Extra reference

Remember that with other verbs you do not have the same choice when there is a change of subject. Look carefully at the following examples:

Sabes muy bien que tu padre se opone a que salgas con Carlos.
You know full well that your father is against you(r) going out with Carlos.

No tengo inconveniente en que aparquen allí.
I don't mind if they park there. / I have no objection to them parking there.

8.6 Negative assertions and statements of uncertainty/ doubt.

No digo que sea malo

- **Using the indefinite mood (the Subjunctive) after statements that emphasise doubt or uncertainty**

  The Subjunctive is found in subordinate clauses that follow *no decir que…. no creer que… dudar que… es dudoso que… no es cierto que… no es verdad que…* and similar phrases. Look carefully at the following examples:

No digo que sea malo.	= I'm not saying he is bad.
No creo que tengas razón.	= I don't think you are right.
Dudo que sea capaz de hacerlo.	= I doubt if he is capable of doing it.
No es cierto que quiera todo.	= It's not true that he wants everything.

  but

Estoy seguro de que vendrá.	= I am sure that he will come.
No cabe duda que te quiere.	= There is no doubt that he loves you.

- **Using the Subjunctive after statements expressing possibility and probability**

  The Subjunctive is always found after **es posible que… es probable que… puede ser que…** .

Es posible que te hayas equivocado. = It's possible you've made a
mistake.

Es probable que venga más tarde. = He will probably come later.

Puede ser que lo hayan perdido. = They might have lost it.

NB: The Subjunctive is not normally used in conjunction with either
probablemente (probably) or **a lo mejor** (perhaps/maybe). This is
because they are not verbal statements but simply adverbs, which
merely qualify the verb stated.

Probablemente vendrán mañana. = They'll probably come tomorrow.

● Using the subjunctive after **quizá(s)** and **tal vez**

The Subjunctive may follow **quizá(s)/tal vez** (perhaps) as long as
they are in front of the verb they are modifying. Note, however, that
the use of the Subjunctive is optional with these words.

Quizá no han/hayan oído la noticia.
Perhaps they haven't heard the news.

Tal vez vendrá/venga esta noche.
Perhaps she will come tonight

Practice (7): Forming phrases of doubt and uncertainty

Translate the following into Spanish:

1 I am not saying you have to do it.
2 I doubt whether she will change her mind. (Use *cambiar de opinión*.)
3 I don't believe that all the changes have been positive.
4 It's not true that she hates you!
5 It's not true that they are going to sack you. (Use *despedir*.)
6 Perhaps they are in the kitchen.
7 They may have made a mistake. (Use *puede ser*.)
8 It will probably rain tomorrow. (Use *es probable*.)
9 I am sure she is French.
10 I don't think she is Spanish.

Extra reference

✦ A useful fixed phrase to learn is, **¡No hay quien lo aguante!** (He's unbearable! / What an insufferable person!).

✦ Another useful phrase is, **no hay nada que…**:
Ahora no hay nada que nos impida casarnos.
Now there is nothing to stop us from getting married.

✦ Be very careful with the phrase, **el hecho de que** (the fact that). Contrary to logic, this phrase is more often followed by the Subjunctive than the Indicative.

8.7 Further uses of the Subjunctive.

**será mejor que te sientes   espero que no vayas a decir…
me extraña que no haya venido   Bendito sea Dios
Que piensen lo que …**

● Impersonal phrases

Normally an Infinitive follows an impersonal phrase.

Es necesario hacerlo.
It's necessary to do it. / It needs to be done.

If there is a change of subject, the normal pattern is to use **que** + the Subjunctive after the impersonal phrase.

No es necesario que lo hagas hoy.
It's not necessary for you to do it today.

Typical impersonal phrases include:

es necesario/es menester/es preciso (que) = it is necessary

más vale/es mejor (que)   = it is better/best (if); … had better…

es imprescindible (que)   = it is essential that

es lástima (que)   = it is a pity that

● **Expressing surprise/hopes/fears and other emotions**

With verbs that express a personal response, the normal pattern is to use **que** + the subjunctive if there is a change of subject.

Me alegro de verte.	= I am pleased to see you.
Me alegro de que hayas venido.	= I am glad you have come.
Lamento no poder verle.	= I regret not being able to see him.

Sólo lamento que mis padres no estén aquí.
I am only sorry that my parents are not here.

Typical verbs in this category include:

esperar (que)	= to hope
temer/tener miedo de (que)	= to fear / to be afraid
lamentar/sentir (que)	= to regret / to be sorry
extrañar a uno/sorprender a uno (que)	= to be surprised that

● **Expressing a wish/suggestion/instruction without a main verb**

In English we tend to use the words **let** or **may** when we want to express a wish/suggestion/instruction without a main verb. In Spanish, the normal pattern is to use **que** + the Subjunctive.

Que no lo toque nadie. = Don't let anyone touch it.

Que no lo sepan ellos. = Don't let them find out.

There are certain fixed phrases which do not require **que**.

Bendita sea Dios. = Thank God! (*Blessed be God!*)

Dios se lo pague. = May God reward you (*for your kindness*).

Practice (8): Recognising sentence patterns

Look carefully at the following sentences. Some of these sentences contain a mistake. Underline the mistake and correct it. Some sentences, however, are correct. Simply tick any sentence that is correct.

1 *Mira, hija, mejor vale que vayas tú misma a comprar el regalo.*

2 *Será mejor si no le digas nada.*

3 *Es preciso avisarle cuanto antes.*

4 *Es preciso que esto acaba pronto.*

5 *No es menester que lo haces ahora mismo.*
6 *Es una gran lástima que se hayan separado.*
7 *Siento decirle que su padre acaba de morir.*
8 *Me extraño que no hayan llegado.*
9 *Espero que no hay más problemas mañana.*
10 *¡Qué aproveche!*
11 *¡Que tengáis buen viaje! Hasta la vista y espero que todo va bien.*
12 *¡Que lo pasas bien! ¡Que te diviertas mucho!*

Extra reference

✦ Developing vocabulary: **esperar**

Note carefully the following:

esperar + **que** + Subjunctive = to hope (that...)
esperar + **a** + **que** + Subjunctive = to wait (for...)
Espero que no vaya a llover. = I hope it is not going to rain.
¿Por qué no esperamos a que vuelva tu padre?
Why don't we wait for your father to get back?

8.8 Indefinite phrases and the Subjunctive

Que piensen lo que quieran

● Indefinite expressions

Look carefully at the following advertisement for a mobile telephone,
paying particular attention to the opening phrase.

**Esté donde esté, tendrá cerca el servicio,
la cobertura y alcance que sólo**
Moviline le puede ofrecer por 85 Pta./día.

— MOVILINE —
Su Servicio de Telefonía Móvil

The opening phrase can be translated as **wherever you are** or **no matter where you are**, and is an example of an indefinite or open-ended statement.

Open-ended/indefinite statements are usually put in the Subjunctive. Look carefully at the following examples:

i) —¿*Dónde lo pongo?*
    —*Donde quieras.* (Where/wherever you like.)

ii) —¿*Cuándo empezamos?*
    —*Cuando quieras.* (When/whenever you like.)

iii) *Puedes coger lo que quieras.* (You can take what/whatever you like.)

iv) *Quieran o no quieran, tienen que hacerlo.* (Whether they like it or not, they have to do it.)

v) *Pase lo que pase, no digas nada.* (Whatever happens, say nothing.)

vi) *Digan lo que digan, no voy a cambiar de opinión.* (No matter what they say, I am not going to change my mind.)

vii) *Dondequiera que vaya, causa problemas.* (Wherever he goes, he causes problems.)

viii) *A cualquier hora que vayas, encontrarás miles de personas rezando o lavándose en el río Ganges.* (At whatever time you go, you will find thousands of people praying or washing themselves in the river Ganges.)

● Indefinite clauses

a) Read the following joke, paying particular attention to the second line.

El copiloto salió de la cabina del avión.

—¿*Hay alguien aquí que crea en la vida futura? —preguntó.*

—¡*Yo creo, yo creo! —exclamó con vehemencia un joven con gafas.*

—¡*Estupendo! —repuso el copiloto—. Vamos a estrellarnos y nos falta un paracaídas.*

In the second line of the joke, the *someone* is indefinite because the co-pilot does not have any particular person in mind. When the object of a main verb is indefinite and there is a second verb involved, the Subjunctive is used. Compare the following two sentences, remembering that in Spanish a distinction is made between what is definite/concrete (the Indicative) and what is indefinite (the Subjunctive).

Buscamos alguien que hable inglés y español.

Conozco a alguien que habla inglés y español.

In the first sentence the speaker does not have a particular person in mind (indefinite). In the second sentence the speaker has a particular person in mind. (definite).

NB: Note that the personal **a** is not used in front of **alguien** when it is indefinite.

b) We saw in section 8.6 that the Subjunctive follows a negative assertion.

This will help you to remember that the Subjunctive is always used with **nadie** (or **ningún/ninguna** + noun) in this type of indefinite construction. And no matter how indefinite the construction, the personal **a** is never omitted in the negative.

No conozco a nadie que hable chino.
I don't know anybody who speaks Chinese.

Practice (9): Recognising open-ended statements

a) Change each verb in brackets into either the Present Subjunctive or the Present Indicative. b) In some of the sentences the personal **a** has been wrongly omitted. Put in the personal **a** where necessary.

1 *Necesitamos un abogado que (entender) alemán.*

2 *Conozco un abogado que (entender) alemán.*

3 *Necesitamos un profesor que (saber) ruso.*

4 *Conozco un profesor que (saber) ruso.*

5 *Busco un hotel que no (ser) muy caro.*

6 *Aquí hay un hotel que no (ser) muy caro.*

7 *Quiero casarme con alguien que (tener) un buen sentido del humor.*

8 *Deseamos algo que (ser) un poquito más elegante.*

9 *No conozco nadie que (poder) ayudarte.*

10 *No conozco nadie que (conducir) tán rápido como tú.*

Progress test 8

Translate the following into Spanish.

1 She said she had had an accident.
2 It had rained during the night.
3 She is not as bad as everybody thinks!
4 He is so fat that he can hardly walk. (Use *caminar*.)
5 I don't have as many problems as she does.
6 My younger sister is bigger than my elder sister.
7 The sooner, the better!
8 This must be the most expensive restaurant in Madrid.
9 There's no better restaurant in Madrid.
10 This is the worst present I have ever received.
11 She is no longer my friend and I don't ever want to see her again.
12 I don't like any of these shirts.
13 I have neither the time nor the desire to see him. (Use ...*de verle*.)
14 He is not allowed to smoke at home.
15 I doubt whether they will come today.
16 Whether you like it or not, you will have to do it.
17 You had better do it now.
18 I am glad they like it.
19 I am surprised they haven't rung.
20 I am looking for a hotel that is not too expensive.

UNIT 9 Imagining, supposing and calculating

Pablo is in an art gallery. Unable to make out the title of a painting he is looking at, he turns to a stranger standing by his side.

Pablo: Perdone usted, ¿podría decirme por favor el título de este cuadro? Es que la letra es muy pequeña. 9.2

Hombre: ¿El título? "Madre e hija". 9.1

Pablo: Es un título un poco raro, ¿no le parece? ¿Dónde está la madre? ¿Dónde está la hija? No veo más que una confusión de colores.

Hombre: Es un retrato simbólico. Los colores mezclados así representan la fluidez de la relación entre la madre y su hija.

Pablo: ¿Qué madre? ¿Qué hija? No veo nada.

Hombre: Se trata de la relación espiritual entre una madre y su hija. Ésa es la razón por la que no se ve ninguna forma concreta. Hay que usar la imaginación para apreciar esta obra. 9.1 9.5 9.4

Pablo: Me imagino que esta "obra" valdrá mucho
              dinero.

Hombre: Un millón de pesetas, más o menos.   9.6

Pablo: ¡Válgame Dios! ¿Hay gente tan tonta que
              pagaría esa cantidad de dinero por una obra   9.2/9.4
              tan ridícula? Ni diez pesetas daría yo por este 9.6; 9.2
              cuadro. No lo aceptaría ni si me lo dieran como 9.4; 9.2; 9.3
              regalo. ¡Es pura basura!

Hombre: A usted no le gusta el arte moderno, ¿verdad?

Pablo: A mí no me gusta que me engañen. Tengo   9.4
              mucho respeto por ciertos artistas modernos,
              pero el pintor de este cuadro está tomando el
              pelo.

Hombre: Si yo fuera el pintor, me sentiría muy ofendido 9.2; 9.4
              por sus palabras.

Pablo: Si yo fuera el pintor, me daría cuenta de que 9.3; 9.2
              no tengo ningún talento artístico y no seguiría 9.2
              engañando al público ni a mí mismo. ¿Qué
              opina usted?

Hombre: Yo soy quien pintó este cuadro.   9.5

9.1 Using **e** instead of **y**.

madre e hija   una madre y su hija

● In front of a word beginning with **i**, **y** changes to **e**.

Hablo inglés y español. = I speak English and Spanish.
Hablo español e inglés. = I speak Spanish and English.

● In front of a word beginning with **hi** (but not *hie*), **y** changes to **e**.

nieve y hielo   = snow and ice
aguja e hilo   = needle and thread

Practice (1): Linking words with either y or e

Complete each gap with either y or e.

1 *Es un chico noble .... incapaz de malicia.*

2 *Abrí la caja .... encontré algo muy raro.*

3 *Tuvieron una discusión sobre las ventajas .... inconvenientes del matrimonio.*

4 *Llovía .... hacía mucho frío.*

5 *Chilló .... hizo un ruido muy extraño.*

6 *Se sentía libre .... independiente.*

7 *Este artista se cree tan grande .... importante.*

8 *En 1992 recibió la Medalla de Oro al Mérito de las Bellas Artes, ... el 24 de noviembre de 1994 le fue concedido el premio Nacional de Cinematografía.*

9 *Se acercó a la puerta .... intentó abrirla.*

10 *No existe ningún gran logro que no sea el resultado de un trabajo constante .... de una espera paciente.*

Extra reference

Note also that **o** (or) changes to **u** when placed before a word beginning with **o** or **ho**.

> *¿Cuál es el número, setenta u ochenta?*
> What is the number, seventy or eighty?

> *De una forma u otra, la mayoría de los animales domésticos son útiles a las personas.*
> In one way or another, most domestic animals are useful to people.

9.2 Forming and using the Conditional tense.

¿podría decirme..? pagaría daría aceptaría me sentiría
me daría cuenta   no seguiría

● Forming the conditional tense

The Conditional tense in Spanish is formed in the same way as the future tense, but with the following endings:

-ía, -ías, -ía, -íamos, -íais, -ían.

In other words, these endings are added to the full Infinitive of most verbs. Those verbs which have an irregular stem for the future tense (See 7.2) will have the same irregular stem for the conditional tense.

Hablar	Tener	Vivir
hablaría	*tendría*	*viviría*
hablarías	*tendrías*	*vivirías*
hablaría	*tendría*	*viviría*
hablaríamos	*tendríamos*	*viviríamos*
hablaríais	*tendríais*	*viviríais*
hablarían	*tendrían*	*vivirían*

● Using the Conditional tense

The conditional tense in Spanish corresponds more or less to the conditional tense in English (*would...*).

a) —*¿Cúanto tiempo?*   = How long?
   —*Una semana, diría yo.* = A week, I would say.

b) *Dijo que no sería lo mismo sin nosotros.*
   He said that it wouldn't be the same without us.

Note that, in reported speech, **iba a** + Infinitive can often be used as an alternative to the Conditional:

Dijo que no iba a ser lo mismo.
He said it wasn't going to be the same.

● Translating **could** / **would** / **should** into Spanish

Be very careful when translating the words **could, would** and **should** into Spanish – these words have a variety of functions in English.

a) **Could**

  i) Could you tell me? = *¿Podría decirme?* (Conditional: *Would it be possible for you to tell me?*)

  ii) I couldn't do it. = *No podía/pude hacerlo.* (Imperfect/Preterite: *I wasn't able to do it/ I didn't manage to do it.*)

b) **Would**

  i) I would like to live in New York. = *Me gustaría vivir en Nueva York.* (Conditional)

  ii) She would hit me for no reason. = *Me pegaba/Solía pegarme sin ninguna razón.* (Imperfect: habitual past action.)

  iii) He wouldn't do it. = *Se negó/negaba a hacerlo.* (Preterite/Imperfect: *wouldn't do it* can mean *refused* to do it.)

c) **Should**

  i) I should like to see them as soon as possible. = *Me gustaría verlos cuanto antes.* (Conditional: **should** is simply more formal than **would**.)

  ii) You should tell him as soon as possible. = *Deberías/Debes avisarle cuanto antes.* (Conditional or Present tense of **deber**: here **should** means *ought to*.)

● The Conditional tense is often used in conjunction with the Imperfect Subjunctive (see 9.3).

Practice (2): Using the Conditional tense in reported speech

Transform each direct statement into reported speech, changing each verb in the future into the conditional and making any other necessary changes.

eg: *—Lo cuidaré bien —prometió Amparo.*
Amparo prometió que lo cuidaría bien.

1 *—Llamaré a Juan y se lo diré —dijo Pedro.*
Pedro dijo que ....

2   —*Trataré de llegar antes de las ocho —dijo Pablo.*
   Pablo dijo ....

3   —*Estoy segura de que a Manuel le gustará el regalo —dijo Mercedes.*
   Mercedes dijo que estaba ....

4   —*Intentaré hacer todo lo posible para arreglar la situación —dijo Isabel.*
   Isabel dijo ....

5   —*No habrá nadie allí —dijo Consuelo.*
   Consuelo........ .

6   —*Lo pensaré —dijo Pepe.*
   Pepe ....

Extra reference

✦   Expressing probability in the past

Just as the Future tense in Spanish is used to express probability
in the present (see 7.2, extra reference), so too the conditional is
used to express probability in the past.

Tendría él unos treinta y siete años.
He must have been around 37 years old.

¿Quién sería? = Who could it be/could it have been?

9.3 Forming and using the Imperfect (or past) Subjunctive.

si me lo dieran como regalo   Si yo fuera

● **The various tenses of the Subjunctive mood**

As you know, the Indicative mood is expressed through various
tenses. The Subjunctive mood is also expressed through a range of
tenses: Present, Present Perfect, Imperfect (past), and Past Perfect.

● **The two forms of the Imperfect Subjunctive**

The Imperfect Subjunctive has two forms: one ending in **-ra**, the
other in **-se**. There is no fundamental difference between the two
forms, although the **-ra** form is slightly more common than the **-se**
form. Apart from a few expressions where **-ra** is preferable to **-se**, it
is entirely up to you which form to use.

● Forming the Imperfect Subjunctive

To form the Imperfect Subjunctive of a verb, you need to know its preterite form. Take the third person plural form of the Preterite and remove the **-ron**.

eg *tuvie(ron) die(ron) cogie(ron)*

Then add: *-ra, -ras, -ra, -ramos, -rais, -ran*
    or: *-se, -ses, -se, -semos, -seis, -sen*

Tener	Dar	Coger
tuviera/tuviese	*diera/diese*	*cogiera/cogiese*
tuvieras/tuvieses	*dieras/dieses*	*cogieras/cogieses*
tuviera/tuviese	*diera/diese*	*cogiera/cogiese*
tuviéramos/tuviésemos	*diéramos/diésemos*	*cogiéramos/cogiésemos*
tuvierais/tuvieseis	*dierais/dieseis*	*cogierais/cogieseis*
tuvieran/tuviesen	*dieran/diesen*	*cogieran/cogiesen*

NB: Note the accent on the first person plural.

● Sequence of tenses:

– The Present/Present Perfect Subjunctive is normally used in conjunction with the present, present perfect and future indicative tenses.

– The Imperfect Subjunctive is normally used in conjunction with the past tenses and the Conditional.

Quiero que se vayan.
I want them to go.

Quería que se fueran/fuesen.
I wanted them to go.

Es preciso que lo hagan.
It is necessary for them to do it.

Era preciso que lo hicieran/hiciesen.
It was necessary for them to do it.

NB: There are occasions, however, when the tenses may be mixed:

Es probable que lo hiciera/hiciese.
It is probable that he did it.

● **Using the Imperfect Subjunctive with si (if)**

Perhaps the most fundamental difference in usage between the Present Subjunctive and the Imperfect Subjunctive occurs with **si** (if). The Present Subjunctive never follows **si**, but the Imperfect Subjunctive does.

Me tratan como si fuera/fuese un idiota.
They treat me as if I were an idiot.

¡Ay, si Pedro me viera/viese ahora!
If only Pedro could see me now!

– A useful phrase to remember is **si no fuera por** (if it were not for...):

Si no fuera por mi padre, no tendríamos nada.
Were it not for my father, we would have nothing.

– An extremely useful word to learn is **ojalá**. Used with the Subjunctive, **ojalá** expresses the idea of *I hope... / If only... / I wish...*

¡Ojalá no vengan!
I hope they don't come.

¡Ojalá fuera/fuese yo tan rico como él!
If only I were as rich as him!

● **Using the Imperfect Subjunctive in conditional statements**

The Imperfect Subjunctive is used in conjunction with the Conditional tense to form conditional statements:

Si yo fuera/fuese rico, compraría un yate.
If I were rich, I would buy a yacht.

Si yo tuviera/tuviese un millón de pesetas, compraría el cuadro.
If I had a million pesetas, I would buy the picture.

● **Using the Imperfect Subjunctive instead of the Conditional tense**

With certain verbs, the Imperfect Subjunctive may be used instead of the Conditional tense. In such cases, the **-ra** form is used.

Yo quisiera/querría	– I would like...
Yo debiera/debería	– I should/ought to...

Practice (3): Becoming familiar with the Imperfect Subjunctive

Match items 1–10 with items a–j.

1 *Yo estaría más contento*

2 *Si fumaras menos,*

3 *Si prestaras más atención en clase,*

4 *Si yo pudiera,*

5 *Ganarías más dinero*

6 *Me acuerdo del incidente*

7 *Si yo fuera profesora,*

8 *Enrique mascaba su cigarro*

9 *Ojalá*

10 *Le pidieron*

a *si trabajaras más.*

b *como si fuera chicle.*

c *que se callara.*

d *aprenderías más.*

e *si tuviera un trabajo más interesante.*

f *trabajaría en el extranjero.*

g *te sentirías mejor.*

h *como si fuera cosa de ayer.*

i *trataría de ser muy paciente con mis alumnos.*

j *tuviéramos una casa más grande.*

Practice (4): Recognising when to use the Imperfect Subjunctive

In the following two passages, change each verb in brackets into either the Conditional tense or the Imperfect Subjunctive.

a) *LO QUE VEN LOS ANIMALES*

Si pudieras ver a través de los ojos de un conejo tú (ver) a un mismo tiempo las cosas situadas delante de ti, a los lados y casi todo lo de detrás.

Pero tú no (distinguir) los colores. Todo (ser) gris y borroso, como la imagen en blanco y negro de un televisor mal sintonizado. Si algo (moverse) detrás de ti, lo (ver) al instante.

Si (tener) los ojos de un halcón, (ver) las cosas de colores, como las ves con tus ojos. Pero lo (ver) todo aumentado. El halcón, volando a 400 metros de altura, puede ver un ratoncillo que corre sobre la hierba.

b) *UNOS PARA OTROS*

Los animales y las plantas se necesitan mutuamente. Si no (ser) por ciertos insectos, muchas plantas no (tener) simientes. Si los animales que se alimentan de plantas no (tener) enemigos que se los comieran a ellos, las plantas (ser) destruidas. Si no (haber) gusanos y otros pequeños animales que viven debajo del suelo, no (haber) tierra buena para las raíces de las plantas. Si no (haber) plantas verdes, no (haber) animales ni personas.

Practice (5): Distinguishing between the Present and Imperfect Subjunctive

Change each verb in brackets into either the Present Subjunctive or the Imperfect Subjunctive.

1 *Pasadas las tres de la madrugada me despertó el teléfono: era Angel. Me sorprendió que me (llamar) a esas horas.*

2 *Me sorprende que Rosaura no (querer) venir con nosotras.*

3 *Por consejo del médico, obligaron al viejo a que (suprimir) toda bebida, (ser) vino o licor.*

4 *El médico le ha prohibido que (beber) alcohol, (ser) vino o licor.*

5 *Pídele que te (explicar) la situación.*

6 *Le pidieron que les (explicar) la situación.*

7 *Dile a Juan que (esperar) diez minutos más.*

8 *Le dijo a Juan que (esperar) diez minutos más.*

9 *Te aconsejo que (cambiar) de trabajo.*

10 *Me aconsejó que (cambiar) de trabajo.*

Extra reference

When **si** means **whether**, it is not followed by the Imperfect Subjunctive.

Yo no sabía si Pedro estaba allí.
I didn't know whether Pedro was there.

Yo no sabía si estaba bromeando o no.
I didn't know whether he was joking or not.

9.4 **Por** or **Para**?

para apreciar   pagaría...por   daría yo por   tengo mucho respeto por   ofendido por

---

● The problem of **por** and **para**

Both **por** and **para** can mean **for** in many contexts, and this naturally leads to some confusion for English speakers. Since this is a fairly complex area, it is best to learn by heart examples that clearly illustrate the main uses of these two words.

● The basic difference between **por** and **para**

The fundamental difference between **por** and **para** is best illustrated by the following questions:

¿Por qué?   =   Why? (*What's the reason?*)

¿Para qué?   =   What for? (*What's the purpose?*)

a) From the question form of the word, we can see that the primary function of **por** is to indicate *a reason* for something. Read the following joke (from a Spanish magazine) and note that the last line can be translated as, "For no particular reason, I just wanted to know."

—*Oiga, ¿qué quiere decir en inglés "why"?*
—*Por que.*
—*No, por nada, por saberlo.*

b) From the question form of the word, we can see that the primary function of **para** is to indicate *purpose*. Read the following joke and note that **para** + Infinitive can be translated as **in order to.../so as to...** .

Un hombre telefoneó a su amigo a las tres de la madrugada.
El aparato sonó y sonó hasta que al fin una voz soñolienta respondió:

—¡Dígame!
—Perdóname —*dijo el primero*— que te haya hecho levantar a estas horas.
—¡No importa! —*contestó el amigo*—. Tenía que levantarme de todas formas para contestar el teléfono.

● Specific functions of **por**

Below you will find six basic uses of **por**:

1 Reason (because of/on account of/out of).

por eso	=	because of that/for that reason
por este motivo	=	for this reason
Lo hace por interés.	=	He does it out of interest.

2 For the sake of / On behalf of.

Lo hice por ella.
I did it for her.

Están dispuestos a morir por la patria.
They are prepared to die for their country.

3 Getting/Fetching/Collecting something or someone.

He venido por mi reloj.
I have come for my watch.

Ha ido por más vino.
He's gone for/to get some more wine.

4 Exchange (in exchange for).

¿Cuánto me das por la bicicleta?
How much will you give me for the bike?

¿Me cambia éste por otro, por favor?
Can you change this one for another one, please?

5 Feelings towards something or someone.

Tengo mucha admiración por ella.
I have a lot of admiration for her.

Tengo gran respeto por Miguel.
I have great respect for Miguel.

6 Duration of time.

Estudió en España por dos años.
He studied in Spain for two years.

Voy por dos semanas.
I am going for two weeks.

sólo por hoy = just for today
sólo por una semana = just for a week

- Don't forget that it is not always necessary to translate **for** into Spanish when it refers to length of time.

Estuvo poco tiempo en Madrid.
He was in Madrid for a short time.

- **Durante** can also be used to translate **for**:

Hubo paz durante treinta años.
There was peace for thirty years.

● As well as meaning **for**, **por** has various other meanings:

a) by

Fue construido por los moros.
It was built by the Moors.

b) through, around, in

por el túnel	= through the tunnel
por allí	= around there
caminar por el parque	= to walk in the park
por la mañana	= in the morning

c) per

el veinte por ciento	= twenty per cent
cien kilómetros por hora	= 100 kilometres per hour
tres veces por semana	= three times per week

● Specific functions of **para**

Below you will find seven basic uses of **para**:

1 **Purpose.**

Estoy estudiando para un examen importante.
I am studying for an important exam.

2 **Destination** (heading for/bound for).

Ya ha salido el tren para Madrid.
The train for Madrid has already left.

3 **Destination** (intended for/meant for).

Este regalo es para ti.
This present is for you.

4 **Suitability.**

Es malo para la salud.
It is bad for your health.

5 **Limit of time (by) / Fixed point of time (for).**

¿Estará listo para viernes?
Will it be ready for/by Friday?

La cita es para el 15 de julio.
The appointment is for 15th July.

6 **Duration of time** (fixed limit).

—¿Para cuántas noches quiere la habitación?
—Para ocho días.

–For how many nights do you want the room?
–For a week.

Practice (6): Recognising when to use **por** or **para**

Complete each gap with either **por** or **para**.

1 *Hace muchos años vivía un hombre al que todo el mundo consideraba un gran maestro y doctor. .... ser tan sabio, todo el mundo le llamaba Buda, que significa "El iluminado".*

2 *En Venecia, Italia, las calles son canales y .... eso no se utilizan automóviles, sino unas barcas especiales que se llaman góndolas.*

3 *Venecia es famosa .... su belleza y su encanto, sus canales y sus góndolas.*

4 *Lo siento, no podemos hacer más .... tu madre.*

5 *—¿........ cuándo es la cita?*
—........ el 18 de este mes.

6 *—¿........ quién es este regalo?*
—........ Consuelo.

7 *—¿........ cuánto tiempo vas a España?*
—Sólo .... ocho días.

8 *—¿Cuánto pagaste .... este libro?*
—No me acuerdo. ¿Por qué quieres saberlo?
—No, ... curiosidad.

9 *El arquitecto que se ha encargado del diseño de la casa nueva tiene una cierta pasión .... las construcciones de estilo andaluz y mediterráneo.*

10 *John Kennedy fue multado con 14.000 pesetas .... haber llevado a su perro al Central Park, de Nueva York, sin su correa correspondiente. Las ordenanzas municipales no permiten que los perros anden sueltos en lugares públicos.*

Extra reference

✦ Developing vocabulary

Por forms part of many common expressions. Look carefully at the following examples:

...o algo por el estilo	= ...or something like that
por desgracia	= unfortunately
por fin	= finally/at last
por lo tanto	= therefore
queda mucho por hacer	= there remains a lot to be done
por poco	= almost/nearly

This last one is an idiomatic phrase which is normally used with a verb in the present tense but referring to the past:

Por poco me caigo.	= I almost fell over.
Por poco se pegan.	= They almost hit each other.
Por poco me muero.	= I nearly died.

9.5 Replacing **que** as a linking word

es la razón por la que   yo soy quien pintó

We have already seen (5.4) that **que**, as a linking word, means **that/which/who**. There are times, however, when **que** is not the most appropriate linking word and an alternative needs to be used.

● **People (who/whom)**

  i) Using **quien/quienes** to replace **que**

  When referring to a person, **que** is not used:
   – after a preposition.
   – in such emphatic phrases as **It was you who...** or **It's Mary who...**

  Instead of **que**, use **quien** (singular) or **quienes** (plural):

La mujer con quien hablabas es una actriz muy famosa.
The woman you were talking to is a very famous actress.
Fue Pedro quien me lo dio.
It was Pedro who gave it to me.

ii) Using **quien/quienes** after a comma

When referring to a person, **que** is usually replaced by
quien/quienes immediately after a comma. This is largely a
question of good style, since the only time it is actually obligatory
to replace **que** after a comma is when the **que** has become
separated by other words from the word it is referring back to.

*Te voy a presentar a Rocío, una amiga mía, quien es de Madrid
también.*
Come and meet Rocío, a friend of mine, who is from Madrid as
well.

iii) Using **el que** or **el cual**

To avoid ambiguity or for emphasis, one can use **el que/la
que/los que/las que** (or alternatively, **el cual/la cual/los
cuales/las cuales**) to replace **que, quien, quienes**.

Es la mujer por la que siento mayor admiración. = *Es la mujer por
quien siento mayor admiración.*

No es mi suegra la que causa los problemas en esta casa. = *No es mi
suegra quien causa los problemas en esta casa.*

– With a short preposition (**a,de,con**), the **el que** form is
preferable to the **el cual** form.

Quiero presentarte a Pedro, al que conozco desde hace quince años.
Quiero presentarte a Pedro, a quien conozco desde hace quince años.

– In general terms, **el cual** is more formal than **el que**.

● Things (which)

i) Replacing **que** with **el que** or **el cual** after most prepositions

When referring to things and following a preposition, **que** is only
used after the prepositions **a, en, de** and **con**. After all other
prepositions, **el que** (or **el cual**) and their feminine and plural

forms are used. (NB: For emphasis, you can also use **el que/el cual** with the short prepositions **a, en, de, con.**)

Ésta es la casa en que nació Cervantes. (or, *...en la que/en la cual...*)
Y ésa es la razón por la cual no me fío de él.
Y ésa es la razón por la que no me fío de él.

– There is no basic difference between **el que** and **el cual** when referring to things, although the **el cual** form is more commonly used after long prepositions (eg *detrás de/delante de/por encima de*).

ii) Using **el que** to replace **que** after a comma

For emphasis and/or to avoid ambiguity, the **el cual** form may be used instead of **que** after a comma.

Me quedan trescientas pesetas, las cuales no quiero gastar.
I have three hundred pesetas left, which I do not want to spend.

Practice (7): Using appropriate linking words

Complete the gaps below in a suitable manner. More than one alternative may be possible.

1 *Es mi marido .... se ocupa de la comida y de los niños cuando me toca trabajar tarde.*

2 *En 1986 Rocío se separó de su marido, José Angel, con .... tuvo dos hijos, José y Felipe.*

3 *En 1993 Rocío contrajo matrimonio con el mejor amigo de José Angel. Tienen una niña, María, ... hoy cumple dos años.*

4 *Habitualmente juego al tenis con mis hijas, ... , además, practican el judo, y la pequeña es campeona de natación.*

5 *Mi hermana que vive en Madrid, ... tiene cuatro gatos y dos perros, piensa casarse con un señor que detesta los animales.*

6 *El hombre a .... di el dinero ha desaparecido.*

7 *Regresó a Washington, la ciudad en .... conoció a su esposa.*

8 *La iglesia tiene una torre muy alta, desde* .... *se ofrece un magnífico panorama.*

9 *Las calles por* .... *pasábamos eran anchas y oscuras.*

10 *Al final de esta calle hay una iglesia, detrás de* .... *se encuentra el colegio que buscáis.*

Extra reference

✦ Translating **those/who**

Note the following expression: *Hay quien dice que...* (There are those who say... / Some people say...).

✦ Translating **when** after time words

After a time word, the normal translation of **when** is **en que**:

el momento en que...	= the moment when..
el día en que...	= the day when..
el año en que...	= the year when..

NB: If you wish, you can omit **en** in this type of phrase:

el día que...	= *el día en que...*

✦ Translating **whose**

Be careful when translating the word **whose**.

i) As a question word, **whose** = **¿de quién?**

¿De quién es este libro?
Whose book is this?

ii) As a linking word, **whose** = **cuyo**.

La señora de Gómez, cuyo marido es el alcalde del pueblo, nos ha invitado a cenar.
Mrs Gómez, whose husband is the Mayor of the village, has invited us to dinner.

9.6 Numerals.

un millón de pesetas   diez pesetas

● 1–99

a) Spelling and formation

Take particular care with numbers 16–30.

1 *uno*	11 *once*	21 *veintiuno*
2 *dos*	12 *doce*	22 *veintidós*
3 *tres*	13 *trece*	23 *veintitrés*
4 *cuatro*	14 *catorce*	24 *veinticuatro*
5 *cinco*	15 *quince*	25 *veinticinco*
6 *seis*	16 *dieciséis*	26 *veintiséis*
7 *siete*	17 *diecisiete*	27 *veintisiete*
8 *ocho*	18 *dieciocho*	28 *veintiocho*
9 *nueve*	19 *dicinueve*	29 *veintinueve*
10 *diez*	20 *veinte*	30 *treinta*

31 *treinta y uno*	60 *sesenta*
35 *treinta y cinco*	70 *setenta*
40 *cuarenta*	80 *ochenta*
48 *cuarenta y ocho*	90 *noventa*
50 *cincuenta*	99 *noventa y nueve*

b) Note that from 31–99, **y** is used to join two numbers.

c) Do not forget that **uno** becomes **un/una** in front of a noun (singular or plural).

Tiene veintiún años.
He is 21 years old.

Tiene cuarenta y un años.
He is 41 years old.

Tengo treinta y una pesetas.
I've got 31 pesetas.

- ## 100–1000

  a) Spelling and formation
  Pay particular attention to 500 and 700.

100 cien(to)	*400 cuatrocientos*
101 ciento uno	*500 quinientos*
110 ciento diez	*600 seiscientos*
120 ciento veinte	*700 setecientos*
200 doscientos	*800 ochocientos*
212 doscientos doce	*900 novecientos*
300 trescientos	*1000 mil*

  b) Note carefully that when a number is joined to 100–1000, no linking word is necessary.

  three hundred <u>and</u> thirty = *trescientos treinta*
  five hundred <u>and</u> fifty-five = *quinientos cincuenta y cinco*

  c) Note that **ciento** becomes **cien** in front of a noun, but not in front of numbers 1-99.

  cien pesetas = 100 pesetas
  ciento veinte pesetas = 120 pesetas

  d) Neither **cien** nor **mil** take the indefinite article (**un/una**).

  cien estudiantes = a hundred students
  tengo mil cosas que hacer = I've got a thousand things to do

  NB: You should also note that neither **otro** nor **cierto** take the indefinite article.

  otro día = another day
  cierta persona = a certain person

  e) Numbers 200–900 have a feminine form (**-as**).
  quinientas pesetas = 500 pesetas

- ## 1001–Two million

  a) Spelling and formation
  1001 mil uno
  1030 mil treinta
  2000 dos mil
  100.000 cien mil
  300.000 trescientos mil
  1.000.000 un millón
  2.000.000 dos millones

b) Note that where in English we use a comma with numbers, in Spanish a full stop is used: twenty thousand = 20,000 (English) *20.000* (Spanish).

c) Note the difference between English and Spanish when designating a year in spoken language:

In 1692 (sixteen ninety-two)
En mil seiscientos noventa y dos.

In 1800 (eighteen hundred)
En mil ochocientos.

In 1996 (nineteen ninety-six)
En mil novecientos noventa y seis.

d) Note very carefully the way **millón** is used:

i) Unlike **cien** and **mil**, **millón** requires a definite article:

a million   = *un millón*

ii) Unlike 'million' in English, **millón** requires **de** when connected with another noun.

a million pesetas   = *un millón de pesetas*
two million pesetas = *dos millones de pesetas*
a million inhabitants = *un millón de habitantes*

● Ordinal numbers (first, second, third...)

a) The numbers we have just been looking at (one, two, three…) are known, grammatically, as *cardinal* numbers. When numbers become adjectival (first, second, third…), they are known as *ordinal* numbers.

It is only worth learning the first ten ordinal numbers in Spanish. For any number over ten (eleventh, twentieth, fiftieth), simply use the appropriate cardinal number (eleven, twenty, fifty).

1st primero	*6th sexto*
2nd segundo	*7th séptimo*
3rd tercero	*8th octavo*
4th cuarto	*9th noveno*
5th quinto	*10th décimo*

b) Ordinal numbers are adjectives and agree with the noun they modify.

mi primera comunión = my first communion

c) Both **primero** and **tercero** drop the final **o** before a masculine singular noun.

el primer piso	= the first floor
el tercer hijo	= the third son

NB: As you already know, the same applies to **malo/bueno/ ninguno/alguno**:

Hace mal tiempo.	= The weather is bad.
Sin ningún problema.	= Without any problems.

d) Note the word order when a cardinal number is used instead of an ordinal when referring to a particular century:

the twentieth century	= *el siglo veinte*
the eighteenth century	= *el siglo dieciocho*

e) When stating a date in spoken Spanish, use **primero** for first and then cardinal numbers thereafter.

Ist July	= *el primero de julio*
2nd May	= *el dos de mayo*
15th November	= *el quince de noviembre*

f) When linking the year with a day and month, use **de**:

El primero de agosto de 1995 = 1/8/95

f) With titles, the definite article (**el/la**) is not used with ordinal numbers:

Elizabeth II (the Second)	= *Isabel Segunda*
Henry VIII (the Eighth)	= *Enrique Octavo*

Practice (8): Using numerals

Read each sentence carefully and then write out each number in full.

1 *Estamos a 16 de mayo.*
2 *20 duros equivalen a 100 pesetas.*
3 *Mi hermano mayor cumple 21 años hoy.*
4 *Hay 28 estudiantes en la clase.*
5 *El jardín tiene 32 metros de largo por 22 de ancho.*
6 *Granada está a unos 48 kilómetros.*

7 *Pesa 75 kilos.*

8 *La velocidad máxima es de 80 kilómetros por hora.*

9 *Cuesta 131 pesetas.*

10 *¿Me puedes prestar 250 pesetas?*

11 *—¿Cuánto es en total? —Son 580 pesetas.*

12 *Un billete de ida y vuelta cuesta 865 pesetas.*

13 *Hay que pagar una multa de 4.000 pesetas.*

14 *Nací en 1982.*

15 *Hay un brandy español que se llama Carlos III.*

16 *¡Le ha tocado el gordo! Ha ganado 30.000.0000 pesetas.*

Extra reference

✦ Measurements/Dimensions

The simplest way to express the height of a person is to use the verb **medir** (to measure).

Alfonso mide 1 metro 80.
Alfonso is 6 ft tall.

The most common way of expressing dimensions is to use **tener + measurement + de + adjective**.

La muralla tiene 20 metros de alto.
The wall is 20 metres high.

El agua tiene 5 metros de profundidad.
The water is 5 metres deep.

¿Cuánto tiene de ancho?
How wide is it?

¿Cuánto tiene de largo?
How long is it?

✦ Note the way 1,2,3… is expressed in the following context. Some children are about to dive into a lake and one of them shouts out:

—Venga, todos al tiempo; cuando yo diga tres. Preparados. A la una; a las dos; y a las tres… .
Come on, everybody at the same time; on the count of three. Ready. One…, two…, and three…!

Progress test 9

Translate the following into Spanish.

1 Carmen and Isabel are my best friends.
2 They said they would help me.
3 They should apologise. (Use *disculparse*)
4 Why do you treat me as if I were a five-year-old child?
5 I wish I was as intelligent as Miguel!
6 If only I had the money to buy that house!
7 I asked them to do it as soon as possible. (Use *pedir*)
8 If they paid more attention in class, they would learn more.
9 She would play the piano better if she practised more.
10 If he stopped smoking, he would feel better.
11 They offered me a thousand pesetas for the picture.
12 And for that reason I don't want to see him.
13 The appointment is for the second of June.
14 It was Marta who helped us most.
15 She was born on the first of August, 1973.

UNIT 10 Regretting the past and speculating about past possibilities

In a concert hall in Sevilla, Ramón has fallen asleep during a performance of Beethoven's 9th Symphony. His girlfriend, Concha, nudges him awake.

Concha: ¡Despiértate, Ramón, por Dios!

Ramón: ¿Qué pasa?

Concha: ¡Estabas roncando! ¡Qué vergüenza!

Ramón: Pero...

Concha: ¡Aquí estamos escuchando una sinfonía de Beethoven interpretada por la Sinfónica de Viena y dirigida por uno de los mejores directores del mundo, y tú <u>te empeñas en echar</u>   10.3 una siesta! Y encima, ¡roncando como un cerdo! <u>Si yo hubiera sabido</u> que te ibas a   10.1 comportar así, <u>no te hubiera invitado a</u>   10.1 <u>acompañarme.</u> <u>Hay gente que habría dado</u>   10.1/10.3 cualquier cosa por obtener una entrada. ¡Estas entradas me costaron un dineral! Hombre, <u>yo</u>   10.1/10.4 <u>hubiera podido invitar a Carmen</u>, por ejemplo: <u>ella sí hubiera apreciado</u> este concierto.   10.1

Ramón: Bueno, bueno, ¡está bien! <u>Francamente</u> <u>si yo</u>   10.2; 10.1
<u>hubiera sabido</u> que el concierto iba a ser tan
pesado, no hubiera aceptado la invitación. No
entiendo de música clásica.

Concha: ¡Podías habérmelo dicho antes! ¿Por qué
aceptaste la invitación si tanto te aburre la
música clásica?

Ramón: Era para complacerte, nada más.

Concha: ¡Vaya manera de complacerme!

Ramón: ¡Vamos, vamos, Concha, cálmate! <u>No tienes que</u> 10.2
<u>gritar tan</u> <u>fuerte</u>. No creo que sea el momento
de discutir, delante de todo el mundo.

Concha: ¡Eres un hombre ignorante, ingrato y mal
educado!

Ramón: ¡Cálmate, por favor! <u>La culpa es mía</u>, lo   10.5
reconozco. Te pido perdón. Anda, Conchita,
¿quieres un beso?

Concha: ¡Suéltame, idiota! ¡Lárgate!

Ramón: ¡No grites, Concha, haz el favor! ¿No notas el
silencio?

Concha: ¿Qué silencio?

Ramón: La orquesta <u>ha dejado de tocar</u>. Todo el mundo 10.3
<u>nos está mirando fijamente</u>. El director de   10.2
orquesta se está encogiendo de hombros.

Concha: ¡Ay, qué pena, madre mía! ¡Ramón, <u>todo esto es</u> 10.5
<u>tu culpa!</u>

Ramón: ¡Un momento! ¿Culpa de qué? Yo estaba
durmiendo, eso sí, pero tú <u>empezaste a</u>   10.3
<u>gritarme</u> <u>en voz alta</u>. La orquesta no ha dejado 10.2
de tocar por mis ronquidos, sino por tus gritos.
<u>O sea</u>, <u>la culpa ahora es tuya</u>.   10.7; 10.5

Hombre: ¿Puedo ayudar en algo?

Concha: ¡<u>Oiga, señor!</u> ¡Me hace el favor de no meter la 10.6
nariz donde no le importa!

Público: ¡¡Olé!! ¡¡Bravo!! *(aplauso)*

10.1 The Past Perfect (Pluperfect) Subjunctive and the Conditional Perfect.

Si yo hubiera sabido... no te hubiera invitado... Hay gente que habría dado... yo hubiera podido invitar...   ella sí hubiera apreciado

---

● **Forming the Past Perfect Subjunctive**

The Past Perfect (or Pluperfect) Subjunctive is formed by the Imperfect Subjunctive of **haber** + Past Participle. Either the **-ra** or **-se** form can be used.

Hablar		
(yo) hubiera hablado or	*hubiese hablado*	= I had spoken
(tú) hubieras hablado	*hubieses hablado*	
(él/ella/Vd) hubiera hablado	*hubiese hablado*	
(nosotros/as) hubiéramos hablado	*hubiésemos hablado*	
(vosotros/as) hubierais hablado	*hubieseis hablado*	
(ellos/as/Vds) hubieran hablado	*hubiesen hablado*	

—*iOjalá lo hubieras dicho antes!* = I wish you had said so before!

NB: Note that we can express these same sentiments without using the Subjunctive: *iPodías haberlo dicho antes!* = You might/could have said so before!

● **Using the Past Perfect Subjunctive**

The main use of the Past Perfect Subjunctive is in conjunction with the Conditional Perfect to form conditional statements that refer to the past.

● **Forming the Conditional Perfect**

The Conditional Perfect is formed by the Conditional form of **haber** + Past Participle.

Comprar
(yo) habría comprado = I would have bought
(tú) habrías comprado
(él/ella/Vd) habría comprado
(nosotros/as) habríamos comprado
(vosotros/as) habríais comprado
(ellos/as/Vds) habrían comprado

● **Using the Past Perfect Subjunctive with the Conditional Perfect**

The Past Perfect Subjunctive and the Conditional Perfect are combined in the following way:

Si yo hubiera sabido que eso iba a suceder, no habría venido.
If I had known that that was going to happen, I would not have come.

● **Using hubiera instead of habría**

Just as the Imperfect Subjunctive can replace the Conditional with certain verbs (see 9.3), so too the **-ra** form of the Past Perfect Subjunctive can be used instead of the Conditional Perfect

Si te hubieras concentrado más, no hubieras hecho tantos errores.
If you had concentrated more, you would not have made so many mistakes.

In other words, it is entirely up to you whether to use **hubiera** or **habría**; just as it is your choice whether to use **hubiera** or **hubiese** after **si**.

Si yo hubiera/hubiese tenido suficiente dinero, lo hubiera/habría comprado.
If I had had enough money, I would have bought it.

● **Translating could have done and should have done**

Particular attention should be paid when forming the conditional perfect with **poder** and **deber**.

i) **Poder**

We can translate **could have done** in three basic ways:

If I had known, I could have invited you.
Si hubiera sabido, habría podido invitarte.
Si hubiera sabido, hubiera podido invitarte.
Si hubiera sabido, podría haberte invitado.

ii) **Deber**

We can translate **should have done** in a variety of ways:

You should/ought to have told me.

Habrías debido decirme.
Deberías haberme dicho.
Debieras haberme dicho.
Has debido decirme.
Debiste decirme.

Practice (1): Becoming familiar with conditional sentences that refer to the past

Match items 1–5 with items a–e.

1 *Si te hubieras levantado más temprano,*

2 *Si no lo hubiera visto con mis propios ojos,*

3 *El accidente no hubiera ocurrido*

4 *Si ella hubiera estudiado más,*

5 *No le hubiera pegado*

a *hubiera aprobado el examen.*

b *si no me hubiera provocado.*

c *no lo hubiera creído.*

d *no habrías llegado tarde al trabajo.*

e *si hubieras conducido con más cuidado.*

Practice (2): Recognising the different ways of expressing conditional sentences referring to the past

Without changing the meaning, rewrite each sentence in a different way.

eg *Si me hubieses dicho que era urgente, lo hubiera hecho para hoy.*
    Si me hubieras dicho que era urgente, lo habría hecho para hoy.

1 *¿Qué hubieras hecho si hubieses estado en la misma situación?*
    = ...

2 *Si me hubiesen avisado con tiempo, yo podría haber hecho algo.*
    = ...

3 *Si hubieran cogido el tren en vez del autobús, no habrían llegado tarde.*

    = ...

4 *Si hubiésemos sabido la verdad, no le hubiéramos tratado de esa manera.*

    = ...

5 *Si hubieras podido vivir en Norteamérica o Europa hace veinte mil años, te habrías creído que estabas en el Polo Norte. La mayor parte de la Tierra estaba cubierta por una gruesa capa de hielo y nieve.*

    = ...

Extra reference

The past perfect subjunctive with **si** is not just used in conjunction with the conditional perfect. It can also be used in conjunction with the ordinary conditional tense.

> *Si no me hubieran/hubiesen ayudado, yo estaría en apuros.*
> If they hadn't helped me (*past*), I would be in great difficulties (*now*).

10.2 Adverbs and adverbial phrases.
francamente   no tienes que gritar tan fuerte   nos está mirando fijamente   en voz alta

- **English and Spanish adverbs**

    Most adverbs in English end in **-ly**. Similarly, a large number of adverbs in Spanish end in **-mente**.

- **Forming an adverb with -mente**

    To form an adverb from an adjective, add **-mente** to the feminine form of the adjective. If the adjective is invariable (eg *alegre, triste*), simply add **-mente**.

    desafortunado – desafortunadamente (unfortunately)

    atento – atentamente (attentively)

    sincero – sinceramente (sincerely)

    triste – tristemente (sadly)

    alegre – alegremente (happily)

- **Retaining accents on adverbs**

    When **-mente** is added to an adjective with an accent, the accent is retained.

    fácil – fácilmente (easily)

    rápido – rápidamente (quickly)

- **Dropping -mente from the first of two adverbs**

    If two adverbs ending in **-mente** are used one after the other, the **-mente** is removed from the first adverb.

    Habló lentamente.
    He spoke slowly.

    Habló lenta y deliberadamente.
    He spoke slowly and deliberately.

● Using adjectives as adverbs

Spanish is more flexible than English in the use of adjectives as adverbs. Note carefully the following examples:

No somos ricos, pero vivimos cómodos.
We are not rich, but we live comfortably.

Vivían juntos y muy felices.
They lived together and very happily.

● Adjectives acting as invariable adverbs

Certain adjectives (masculine singular form) function as invariable adverbs in fixed contexts.

No hablaron muy claro.
They didn't speak very clearly.

¿Este tren va directo a Madrid?
Does this train go directly to Madrid?

Trabajamos duro.
We work(ed) hard.

No grites tan fuerte.
Don't shout so loudly.

Caminamos rápido para casa.
We walked quickly home.

● Note the following adverbs:

badly = *mal*
well = *bien*
quickly = *de prisa/deprisa* (one word or two)
slowly = *despacio*

● Avoiding the **-mente** form

More often than not, the **-mente** form is avoided in Spanish by the use of adverbial phrases:

violentamente = con violencia (**con** + noun)

muy bruscamente = de una manera muy brusca/de un modo muy brusco

● **Common adverbial phrases**

The most common adverbial phrases are formed with the following prepositions: **a, de, en, con, sin**. (See also 9.4 for phrases with **por**). Study carefully the following examples:

1) **a**

a ciegas – blindly
a gatas – on all fours
a oscuras – in the dark
a toda prisa/velocidad – at full speed
a menudo – often
a escondidas – secretly (*without being seen*)

2) **de**

de esta manera/forma; de este modo – in this way
de buena gana – willingly
de mala gana – unwillingly
de vez en cuando – occasionally
de pronto/de repente – suddenly
de nuevo – again
de costumbre – usually
de rodillas – kneeling

3) **en**

en voz alta – loudly/aloud
en voz baja – softly
en vano – in vain
en seguida – immediately/at once
en confianza – confidentially

4) **con**

con alegría – happily/joyfully
con ironía – ironically
con lágrimas – tearfully
con cuidado – carefully
con anticipación – in advance

5) **sin**

sin prisa – slowly
sin miedo – unafraid
sin reserva – unreservedly

Practice (3): Forming adverbs

Change each adjective in brackets into an adverb ending in **-mente**.

1 *Estaban comiendo (tranquilo).*
2 *Cantaban (alegre).*
3 *Lloraba (amargo).*
4 *Le habló (cortés).*
5 *Me miraba (triste).*
6 *Le escuchamos (atento).*
7 *Durmió (profundo) toda la noche.*
8 *El caballo galopaba (rápido).*
9 *Lo hacían (callado).*
10 *Miraban (constante) por la ventana.*

Practice (4): Forming adverbial phrases with **con**

Translate the following adverbs into Spanish. In each case, use **con**.

1 calmly
2 patiently
3 carefully
4 enthusiastically
5 affectionately

Practice (5): Recognising adverbial phrases

Complete each gap with **a, de**, or **con**.

1 *—¡Tengo sed! —dijo .... voz alta.*
2 *Vio .... horror que el otro tenía una navaja en la mano.*
3 *Se sentaron .... silencio.*
4 *Apareció un hombre vestido .... un modo muy extraño.*
5 *Se miraron .... asombro el uno al otro.*
6 *El tren iba .... toda velocidad.*
7 *Se puede sacar las entradas .... anticipación.*
8 *Tan espesa era la niebla que tuvimos que bajar la colina .... ciegas.*
9 *Lo hizo, pero .... mala gana.*
10 *Me abrazó .... alegría.*

Practice (6): Recognising special adverbial patterns

Without changing their form, complete the statements below with the following words:

contentos   fuerte   rápido   cómodo   atento   claro   mal

1 *¿Puedes hablar más ....? Es que no te entiendo.*

2 *Jugaban .... en el jardín.*

3 *El viento soplaba tan .... que casi no podíamos caminar.*

4 *Las cosas me han ido muy ....*

5 *Les escuchó muy ....*

6 *¿Por qué no coges el tren? En tren, vas .... y ....*

10.3   Verb + infinitive.

**te empeñas en echar   no te hubiera invitado a acompañarme
ha dejado de tocar   empezaste a gritarme**

● **Which preposition?**

When an Infinitive follows a verb, a preposition is often required as a link word. Unfortunately, there is no easy way of remembering which preposition goes with which verb. Accordingly, the most basic verbs + preposition should be learnt by heart.

It is equally important to know which verbs do not need a preposition. Study very carefully the groupings below.

● **Verbs followed by a + Infinitive.**

a) **beginning/starting**

    comenzar a/empezar a/echar(se) a = to begin/start to do/doing

b) **learning/teaching**

    aprender a/enseñar a = to learn how to/to teach how to

c) **movement**

    ir a/venir a/apresurarse a = to go to/to come to/to hasten to

d) **helping/persuading/encouraging/forcing/inviting**

ayudar a/persuadir a/animar a = to help to/to persuade to/ to encourage to

forzar a/verse obligado a/obligar a/invitar a = to force to/to be forced to/to oblige to/to invite to

e) **deciding/refusing** (reflexive verbs)

decidirse a/negarse a = to decide to/to refuse to

f) **miscellaneous**

acertar a = to succeed in/to manage to

atreverse a = to dare to

renunciar a = to give up

volver a = to do something again

- Verbs followed by **de** + infinitive.

a) **stopping/finishing/ending**

dejar de/parar de/cesar de = to stop/cease

b) **emotions**

alegrarse de = to be glad to

arrepentirse de = to regret

cansarse de = to be tired of/to grow weary of

quejarse de = to complain about

tener ganas de = to feel like

c) **memory**

acordarse de = to remember to

olvidarse de = to forget to

d) **miscellaneous**

tratar de = to try to

tener el derecho de = to have the right to

tener la intención de = to have the intention of

● Verbs followed by **en** + Infinitive.

interesarse en	= to be interested in
consistir en	= to consist of
insistir en/empeñarse en	= to insist on
persistir en	= to persist in
pensar en	= to think about (consider)
tardar en	= to take time in
hacer bien en	= to be quite right to
hacer mal en	= to be wrong to
vacilar en	= to hesitate to
esforzarse en	= to strive to/try hard to
convenir en/quedar en	= to agree to

● Verbs followed by **con** + Infinitive.

amenazar con	= to threaten to
contentarse con	= to be happy to (*to rest content with*)
soñar con	= to dream of

● **Verbs that do not take a preposition when followed by an Infinitive.**

a) **verbs of perception** (*escuchar/oír/ver/sentir*)

Le oí bajar las escaleras. = I heard him come down the stairs.

b) **making/ordering/permitting/advising**

hacer/permitir/mandar/dejar/impedir/prohibir/aconsejar
to make/permit/order/let/prevent/forbid/advise

No me dejaron salir. = They didn't let me go out.

c) **manage to**

lograr/conseguir = to manage to/to succeed in

d) **miscellaneous**

pensar hacer algo = to think of doing something (*plan/intention*)

esperar hacer algo = to hope to do something

decidir hacer algo = to decide to do something

intentar/procurar hacer algo = to try to do something

Practice (7): Becoming familiar with verbs + Infinitive

Complete the following sentences by adding the missing preposition. If no preposition is required, mark the gap with a cross (*X*).

1 *Lograron .... llegar a la cumbre.*

2 *Amenazó .... llamar a la policía.*

3 *Hiciste bien .... salir temprano.*

4 *Me canso .... viajar tanto.*

5 *¿Cuándo vas ... aprender .... conducir?*

6 *Se negó .... hacerlo.*

7 *Tengo ganas .... comer un chocolate.*

8 *¡No te olvides .... limpiar el horno!*

9 *Trataron .... engañarme.*

10 *¡Procura .... no hacer un ruido!*

11 *Quedaron .... verse a las ocho.*

12 *Hiciste mal .... hacer esa pregunta.*

13 *Oímos .... entrar a María.*

14 *Se echó .... llorar.*

15 *No se atrevió .... decírselo.*

16 *Insistieron .... ayudarnos.*

17 *Hay que animarle .... hacer más ejercicio.*

18 *Tardaron .... llegar.*

19 *Se pusieron .... correr.*

20 *Me forzaron .... abrir la caja fuerte.*

10.4 The personal **a**.

Yo hubiera podido invitar a Carmen

● **The use of the personal a**

The personal **a**, which has no equivalent in English, must be used before any person noun that is the object of a verb.

Quiero invitar a Carmen.
I want to invite Carmen.

Vi a Pedro ayer.
I saw Pedro yesterday.

● **Introducing an extra indirect object pronoun**

Note that no extra indirect object pronoun (**me,te,le…**) is used when the **a** is personal. If, however, the **a** is acting as a straightforward preposition with a particular meaning, then it is normal to use an extra indirect object pronoun.

Le dije a Carmen que…
I said to Carmen that…

Se lo di a Pedro.
I gave it to Pedro.

● **The personal a and tener**

The personal **a** is not normally used with **tener**.

Tengo dos hermanos.
I have got two brothers.

Tengo pocos amigos.
I have got few friends.

However, the personal **a** can be used with **tener** if a particular emphasis is being made.

Hombre, no estás solo. ¡Tienes a tu familia! ¡Tienes a tus amigos!
Come on, you are not alone. You've got your family! You've got your friends!

● **The personal a and animals**

The personal **a** may be used in front of animals, especially if referring to a pet.

¿Por qué maltratas a tu perro? = Why do you mistreat your dog?

● **The personal a with definite people or groups of people**

Any word that represents a person or a group of people takes the personal **a**, except if the word is indefinite. (See also 8.8)

Busco un profesor privado. = I am looking for a private teacher.

Necesito un abogado. = I need a lawyer.

● **The personal a with numbers**

The personal **a** is optional in front of numbers, except if there is a particular personal focus on the noun.

La policía ha detenido (a) cien estudiantes.
The police have detained one hundred students.

La policía ha detenido a los dos hombres que trataron de robarme.
The police have detained the two men who tried to rob me.

● **The personal a with hay and ser**

The personal **a** does not follow **hay** or **ser**.

Hay mucha gente aquí. = There are a lot of people here.

Son mis mejores amigos. = They are my best friends.

● **Omitting the personal a**

The personal **a** is omitted in the first part of a sentence if there is any possibility of confusion with **a** meaning **to** in the second half of the sentence.

Presenté Carmen a Ramón. = I introduced Carmen to Ramón.

Prefiero Pedro a Miguel. = I prefer Pedro to Miguel.

but

¿A quién prefieres, a Pedro o a Juan?
Who do you prefer, Pedro or Juan?

Practice (8)

Insert **a** where necessary in the sentences below.

1 *Trato de visitar mi abuela todos los días.*

2 *Voy a ver mi hermano, Juan, esta tarde.*

3 *Oye, Luis, ¿por qué no ayudas tu madre más a menudo?*

4 *Lo siento, señora; no conozco este señor.*

5 *Te digo Juan; hay que llamar la policía.*

6 *Tengo que ir al aeropuerto a recoger mi suegra.*

7 —*!Oiga, camarero! ¿Sirve usted cangrejos?*
   —*Tome asiento, señor. Aquí servimos todo el mundo.*

8 *No hay que comparar Juana con Isabel. Ellas son totalmente distintas.*

9 *Isabel quiere mucho su hermano.*

10 *¿Quién quieres más, tu hijo o tu hija?*

Extra reference

There are two further uses of **a** that you should particularly note.

✦ **a** is placed in front of any expression of *distance*.

> *La piscina está a dos kilómetros de mi casa.*
> The swimming-pool is two kilometres from my house.

✦ **a** can mean *from*.

> *El policía le quitó el pasaporte al estudiante.*
> The policeman took the passport from the student.

> *Le compré el coche a mi hermano.*
> I bought the car from my brother.

10.5 Tu, tuyo or el tuyo?

la culpa es mía   todo esto es tu culpa   la culpa ahora es tuya

● Possessive adjectives

In front of a noun, the following possessive adjectives are used:

mi(s)	= my
tu(s)	= your
su(s)	= his/her/its/your
nuestro (a/os/as)	= our
vuestro (a/os/as)	= your
su(s)	= their/your

These words agree with the noun they modify.

mis zapatos	= my shoes
nuestros amigos	= our friends

In the case of **su(s)**, ambiguity can be avoided by using **de +
él/ella/usted/ellos/ellas/ustedes.**

her house	= *la casa de ella/su casa (de ella).*
his books	= *los libros de él/sus libros (de él)*

● Possessive pronouns

Pronouns are used instead of nouns. Just as there are subject and
object pronouns, so too there are possessive pronouns.

In Spanish, possessive pronouns have two forms (with or without the
definite article):

(el) mío, (la) mía, (los) míos, (las) mías = mine
(el) tuyo, (la) tuya, (los) tuyos, (las) tuyas = yours
(el) suyo, (la) suya, (los) suyos, (las) suyas = his/hers/its/yours
(el) nuestro, (la) nuestra, (los) nuestros, (las) nuestras = ours
(el) vuestro, (la) vuestra, (los) vuestros, (las) vuestras = yours
(el) suyo, (la) suya, (los) suyos, (las) suyas = theirs/yours

- A possessive pronoun agrees with the noun it refers to.

- The definite article is not used after **ser**.
  ¿De quién son estos libros? ¿Son míos o tuyos?
  Whose books are these? Are they mine or yours?

- The definite article is not used when the possessive pronoun comes immediately after a noun. Note carefully how each of the following phrases is translated:
  unos amigos míos   = some friends of mine
  una prima tuya   = a cousin of yours
  un pariente nuestro = a relative of ours

- The definite article is used *at all other times*.
  Esta corbata no es mía. ¿Quién ha cogido la mía?
  This tie isn't mine. Who has taken mine (my one)?
  —¿Voy en mi coche o en el tuyo?
  Shall I go in my car or yours?
  —Mejor en el mío.
  Better in mine.

- In the case of **(el) suyo, (la) suya, (los) suyos, (las) suyas**, ambiguity can be avoided by simply using **de** + **él/ella/usted/ellos/ellas/ustedes**.
  This jacket is yours, isn't it?
  Esta chaqueta es suya, ¿verdad? / Esta chaqueta es de usted, ¿verdad?

Practice (9): Using possessive adjectives and pronouns

1) Use the correct form of **mi** or **mío** to complete the sentences below.

   a —........ *padres no pueden venir a la reunión.*
      —........ *tampoco.*

   b —*Estos lápices son* ....
      —*No, son* .... *lápices.*

   c —*¿Qué quieres, hija* .... ?
      —*Quiero ir al cine con unas amigas* .... , *pero no tengo dinero.*

2) Use the correct form of **tu** or **tuyo** to complete the sentences below.

   a —*Me gusta* .... *dibujo.*
       —........ *es mucho mejor. Yo no sé dibujar.*

   b —*¿Dónde están* .... *guantes?*
       —*No sé. ¿Puedo usar* .... *?*

   c —*Ésta es mi bolsa.* .... *está debajo de la mesa.*

3) Use the correct form of **nuestro** to complete the sentences below.

   a —........ *teléfono no funciona.*
       —........ *tampoco.*

   b —........ *profesora de español es de Madrid.*
       —........ *es inglesa, pero ha vivido muchos años en España.*

10.6 Señor or el señor?

¡Oiga, señor!

● **Using or omitting the definite article (él/la/los/las) before a noun**

Note very carefully how the definite article in Spanish is either used or omitted in the following situations:

● **Before the title of a person**

The definite article (**el/la/los/las**) is used before the title of a person (except when addressing that person directly).

La señora de Juanco es muy simpática.
Mrs Juanco is very nice.

Buenos días, señora Juanco.
Good morning, Mrs Juanco.

(The definite article is not used with **don/doña**.)

● **Before proper nouns**

The definite article is not usually used with proper nouns, except if the noun is qualified by an adjective.

Aquí está Pedro. = Here is Pedro.

¡El pobre Pedro! = Poor Pedro!

- **With languages**

  With regard to languages, the following rules apply:

  a) A language will always retain the definite article if it is the subject of a verb.

     El inglés es difícil.

  b) The definite article is usually omitted after **hablar. saber**, **en**, and **de** (meaning *of*).

     Hablo ruso.
     I speak Russian.

     ¿Sabes francés?
     Do you know (any) French?

     ¿Puedes escribirlo en español?
     Can you write it in Spanish?

     Un curso de inglés.
     An English course.

  c) The definite article is optional after such verbs as **aprender, estudiar, escribir, enseñar**.

     Estoy estudiando (el) español.
     I am studying Spanish.

- **With the days of the week**

  The definite article is also used with the days of the week (when we want to say **on** a particular day) and in expressions with *next* or *last*.

el lunes = on Monday (*but Hoy es lunes.*	= Today is Monday.)
los lunes	= on Mondays
el lunes que viene/el lunes próximo	= next Monday
el lunes pasado	= last Monday

Practice (10): Recognising when to use and when to omit the definite article

In the gaps below, put in **el, la** or **los** where necessary. If an article is not required, write **✗** in the space.

1 —¿*Puedo hablar con* .... *señor Juanco?*
   —........ *señor Juanco está ocupado.*

2 *Buenos días,* .... *señor Sánchez.*

3 .... *doctor Ramos está enfermo.*

4 *Hola,* .... *Luis.*

5 .... *pobre María nunca tiene suerte.*

6 .... *señores Gómez viven en el segundo piso.*

Practice (11): Using or omitting the definite article

In the gaps below, put in **el** or **la** where necessary. If an article is not required, write **✗** in the space.

1 ¿*Hablas* .... *chino?*

2 *Mi padre da clases de* .... *francés.*

3 *Me puedes escribir en* .... *inglés si no quieres escribirme en* .... *español.*

4 .... *español no es tan difícil.*

5 *Creo que* .... *italiano es más fácil de aprender que* .... *griego.*

6 *Voy a visitarla* .... *domingo próximo.*

7 *Tenemos un examen* .... *semana que viene.*

8 *Hoy es* .... *sábado.*

9 ¿*Qué piensas hacer* .... *año que viene?*

10 *Voy a comprar el vestido* .... *miércoles.*

Extra reference

Nouns in apposition do not take the definite article.

a) *La capital de Francia es París.*

but

París, capital de Francia, es una ciudad muy interesante.

b) *—¿Qué fecha es? —Es el catorce de julio.*

but

—¿Qué fecha es? —Es martes, catorce de julio.

10.7 O sea... *(reference only)*

O sea, la culpa ahora es tuya.

- The straightforward translation of the idiomatic phrase **o sea** is **that is to say** or **in other words**. It can also be translated as **or rather** or **what I mean is...**

  When you go to Spain, you will hear this phrase often. Just as some English people use the word *actually* every two or three sentences, so too you will hear **o sea** over and over again.

Progress test 10

Translate the following into Spanish.

1   If she hadn't seen it with her own eyes, she wouldn't have believed it.
2   If he had driven more carefully, the accident would not have happened.
3   If we had left five minutes earlier, we would not have missed the train.
4   If you had told me before, I could have done something.
5   You shouldn't read in the dark.
6   He spoke softly in order not to wake the others.
7   They were playing peacefully in the garden.
8   Sometimes he behaves very strangely.
9   They refused to give the money to Pedro.
10 He insists on speaking with the owner.
11 We managed to persuade him to come with us.
12 We agreed to meet at six.
13 I saw Teresa yesterday.
14 We need a doctor.
15 I am going to France next month because I want to learn French.

Answer section

Unit 1

Practice 1

¡Qué bien cantas! ¡Qué bebé tan lindo! ¡Qué suerte tienes! ¡Qué hombre más perezoso! ¡Qué fuerte eres! ¡Qué felices parecen! ¡Qué chica más guapa! ¡Qué ojos más bonitos! ¡Qué frío hace aquí dentro! ¡Qué ejercicio más fácil!

Practice 2

1) b 2) c 3) a 4) c 5) b 6) c

Practice 3

1 Dónde 2 Adónde 3 Por dónde 4 De qué 5 En qué 6 Cuánto 7 Cuántos 8 Cuál 9 Qué 10 De quién 11 Quién 12 Para qué 13 A qué 14 Cómo 15 Cuándo 16 Por qué

Practice 4

¿A cuánto son/Cuánto cuestan estas manzanas?
Y, ¿ésas?
Sí, ésas verdes.
Y aquellas rojas, ¿cuánto valen?
Eso no es cierto/verdad.
¡Esto es ridículo!
Eso no es mi problema.

Practice 5

1 A mí me gusta la música clásica. 2 ¿A ti te gustan los perros?
3 A Fernando no le gusta el té. 4 A ellos no les gusta bailar.
5 ¿Os gusta este vestido?

Practice 6

1 ¿A ti te gusta este disco?
2 Me gusta jugar al ajedrez en mis ratos libres.
3 A mi hermana le gusta tomar el sol, pero a mí no.
4 correct
5 A Paco no le gusta estudiar.
6 correct
7 A mi abuelo no le gusta salir; prefiere quedarse en casa. En cambio, mi abuela se aburre en casa; a ella sí le gusta salir.
8 A muchas personas no les gustan las arañas.
9 ¿Cuál te gusta más, éste o ése?
10 correct

Practice 7

1 Me parece que va a llover. 2 No me parece una buena idea. 3 Pilar no se parece mucho a su madre. 4 ¿Qué tal te parece este disco? 5 Me parece que sí. 6 Con tanto maquillaje en la cara, pareces un payaso. 7 A mí no me parece tan guapo aquel chico. 8 Me parece muy pesado este libro. 9 ¿Qué te parece si vamos al cine esta tarde? 10 ¡Me parece poco dinero!

Practice 8

(l) I will call her. **(2)** I'm coming, mum/mother! **(3)** She's just coming. **(4)** Do you feel like/fancy going out..? **(5)** Where are we going/shall we go? **(6)** If you like. **(7)** What's on? **(8)** It starts.. **(9)** (At) what time shall we meet/see each other? **(10)** where shall we meet?

Practice 9

1 I can't find them **2** is coming **3** Can/Will you help me **4** Are you going   Do you want   Could you bring me **5** comes   are you going   what are you having? **6** What are you doing   Can you do me a favour? **7** What does your father do? **8** I'll bring it..

Progress test 1

1 ¡Qué sorpresa! **2** ¡Qué bien bailan! **3** ¡Qué hombre más estúpido!/¡Qué hombre tan tonto! **4** ¿Adónde vas, Enrique? **5** ¿Quién es aquella chica? **6** (A mí) me gustan estos zapatos. **7** No me gusta este vestido, pero me gusta ése. **8** A mi hermano le gusta ese disco. **9** A él no le gusta bailar. **10** ¿Qué es esto? **11** Eso sí que es cierto/verdad. **12** ¿Qué quiere decir esto? **13** ¿Qué tal te parece José? **14** Me parece simpático./Me cae bien. **15** Me parece muy caro este hotel.

UNIT 2

Practice 1

1) trabajo Llevo   cubre   va   puede   lleva = b
2) podemos   reparamos   es   corremos   ganamos = c
3) consiste   hay   salimos = a
4) doy   dirijo   soy   ocurre = b

Practice 2

debes Necesito prometo dices doy vas prometes cumples puedo tienes vale sé voy voy crees creo soy conozco

Practice 3

1 Hago **2** digo **3** salgo **4** oigo **5** Veo **6** cojo **7** conozco **8** traigo **9** pongo **10** tengo

Practice 4

(1) es **(2)** soporta **(3)** Abandona **(4)** acepta **(5)** propone **(6)** tiene **(7)** son **(8)** rivalizan **(9)** necesita

Practice 5

1 c **2** g **3** a **4** b **5** i **6** h **7** j **8** d **9** f **10** e

Practice 6

1 b **2** a **3** a **4** b **5** b **6** b **7** b **8** b **9** a **10** b

Practice 7

1 frías **2** frío **3** mucha **4** mucho **5** el **6** éxito **7** sueño **8** ganas **9** miedo **10** razón **11** prisa **12** que **13** gracia **14** años **15** culpa **16** nada **17** tiene **18** suerte

Practice 8
1 a) se esconde b) esconde 2 a) enoja b) se enoja 3 a) cuida b) se cuida
4 a) cortarte b) cortas 5 a) cenan b) se cena 6 a) comes b) se come
7 a) bañaros b) baño 8 a) se necesitan b) necesita

Practice 9
se necesitan se recogen se ponen se clasifican se les quita se llevan se mezcla

Practice 10
se saca forman se deposita parecen se bate se unen forman se juntan
se transforma se saca se llama

Progress test 2
1 No fumas, ¿verdad? (Usted) no fuma, ¿verdad? 2 traigo; puedo; hago; veo; oigo; digo; salgo; vengo, cojo; sé; conozco. 3 damos; vendemos; podemos; queremos; tenemos; abrimos; sufrimos. 4 Tiene(s) los pantalones sucios.
5 (Ella) tiene los ojos azules. 6 Tiene dolor de cabeza. 7 No tengo dinero.
8 No tengo mucha hambre. 9 Tengo mucho sueño. 10 No tenemos prisa.
11 No tenemos nada que declarar. 12 Nunca se enfada. 13 ¿A qué hora se abre el banco? 14 ¿Por qué no te quitas la chaqueta?/¿Por qué no se quita (usted) la chaqueta? 15 Se habla inglés aquí.

UNIT 3

Practice 1
a) 1 ¿Cuánto tiempo llevamos esperando el autobús? 2 ¿Llevas mucho tiempo aquí? 3 Llevo casi dos años sin comer carne. 4 Lleva más de tres años sin trabajar.
b) 1 ¿Desde hace cuánto tiempo viven en Valladolid? 2 Viven en Segovia desde hace seis años. 3 Tengo este coche desde hace tres meses. 4 Somos amigos desde hace quince años. 5 No fumo/No he fumado desde hace nueve meses.
c) 1 ¿Hace mucho (tiempo) que están aquí? 2 Hace mucho (tiempo) que no voy al teatro. 3 Hace diez años que no la veo/no la he visto.

Practice 2
1 conozco 2 Conoce conozco sé Conoce sé 3 Conoce conozco 4 sabe
5 sabemos 6 sabe

Practice 3
1 Sabes 2 Puedes 3 Puedes 4 Sabes 5 Puedes 6 Puedes 7 Sabes 8 Sabes
9 Sabes 10 Puedes

Practice 4
1 b 2 a 3 b 4 c 5 b 6 c 7 a 8 b 9 c 10 b 11 b 12 c

Practice 5
1 g 2 c 3 e 4 f 5 a 6 h 7 d 8 b

Practice 6
pido te niegas encuentras sigues me encuentro me siento duele te acuestas quiero me acuerdo se cierra sirve piensas vuelves entiendes

Practice 7

1 e (cuesta) **2** d (sueña) **3** a (sueles) **4** f (seguimos) **5** c (advierten) **6** b (Mide)

Progress test 3

1 ¿Cuánto tiempo llevan esperando? **2** Conozco a Pedro desde hace dos años. **3** Hace mucho que no te veo./Hace mucho que no le veo a usted. **4** Acaban de llegar. **5** ¿Sabes/Sabe (usted) tocar la guitarra? **6** Yo sé la verdad. **7** Les hace falta dinero. **8** Hace tanto calor aquí. **9** ¿Puedo hacer una pregunta? **10** Ella no hace caso a su madre. **11** Siempre hace el ridículo/el tonto. **12** Lo bueno es que no tenemos que pagar. **13** empiezo; pierdo; vuelvo; prefiero; duermo; nieva; llueve. **14** No se siente/se encuentra bien. **15** ¿Qué piensa(s) hacer?

UNIT 4

Practice 1

(1) es **(2)** Es **(3)** es **(4)** Es **(5)** estoy **(6)** es **(7)** está **(8)** Es

Practice 2

1 es **2** está está **3** es **4** es **5** está **6** es **7** está **8** está **9** Es **10** está **11** es **12** estás **13** es **14** están **15** es **16** está **17** es **18** es soy **19** está está **20** es Es **21** es Son **22** está Estoy **23** ser **24** está **25** estoy **26** estás **27** Está soy **28** Estás **29** sois **30** estáis

Practice 3

1 Qué **2** Qué **3** Cuál **4** Cuál **5** Qué **6** Cuál **7** Qué **8** Cuál **9** Qué **10** Cuáles **11** qué **12** Qué **13** Cuál **14** Cuál **15** Cuál **16** Cuál **17** Cuál **18** Qué

Practice 4

1 diciendo **2** tomando **3** poniendo **4** buscando **5** trabajando **6** durmiendo **7** siguiendo **8** leyendo **9** escribiendo **10** conduciendo **11** pidiendo **12** lloviendo construyendo

Practice 5

1 ¿Quién es la chica sentada a la mesa? **2** Llegan/Van a llegar mañana a las diez. **3** Están charlando en la cocina. **4** ¿Por qué está ladrando el perro? **5** ¿Ves a Pedro? Está asomado a la ventana. **6** Estás tosiendo mucho. ¿Estás bien? **7** Aquel chico/muchacho apoyado en la pared es el novio de Andrea. **8** Voy a Francia mañana y no vuelvo hasta la semana que viene. **9** Está tumbada en el suelo, haciendo (sus) ejercicios. **10** ¿Por qué estás de pie? ¿Por qué no te sientas?/¿Por qué está (usted) de pie? ¿Por qué no se sienta?

Practice 6

1 Estamos haciéndolo. **2** Están revisándolo. **3** Estoy contándolos. **4** Quiero terminarlo cuanto antes. **5** ¿Estás copiándolo? **6** Estamos escuchándole. **7** Están cambiándolas. **8** Están esperándonos. **9** Voy a decirte una cosa. **10** Estamos examinándola. **11** Estoy leyéndolo. **12** Está lavándose las manos. **13** Voy a lavarme las manos. **14** Los niños están bañándose en el río. **15** No estamos tocándolo. **16** No están mirándonos. **17** Tienen que pagarnos. **18** ¡Están rompiéndolo! **19** Vamos a pintarlo. **20** Estoy reparándolo.

Practice 7

1 Me han suspendido en matemáticas. **2** Ella se ha portado muy bien. **3** No me han escrito. **4** Nunca he montado a caballo. **5** ¡Me he quemado! **6** ¿Qué tal lo has pasado? **7** Lo hemos pasado muy bien. **8** Me he divertido mucho. **9** Me he torcido el tobillo. **10** ¿Qué ha comprado Ana?

Practice 8

a) ha parado   Ha habido   ha ocurrido
b) ha dicho   te has decidido   he dimitido   han puesto   he querido   he ahorrado
c) Se ha ido   se ha acostado   ha tocado
d) Has leído   ha enseñado   ha abierto   ha hecho
e) Has hecho   Has arreglado   Has dado   Te has lavado   Has puesto

Progress test 4

1 ¿Cómo es Camilo? **2** ¿De dónde es Núria? **3** ¿Cómo están tus padres? **4** Mi madre es actriz. A mi parecer, es una gran actriz. **5** ¿Está casada o es soltera? **6** ¿Cuál es el problema? ¿Por qué estás de mal humor? **7** ¿Qué estás leyendo? ¿Es interesante? **8** No nos está escuchando./No está escuchándonos. ¿Está durmiendo? **9** Se están levantando. **10** Se han levantado. **11** ¡Me han robado! **12** Le han despedido. **13** ¿Ha vuelto Pedro? **14** No la hemos visto. **15** ¡Me han engañado!

UNIT 5

Practice 1

a) vivía   tenía   podía   servían   estaba   era   parecía   Amaba   llamaba   Pasaba   abría   guardaba   estaba
b) acababa   lloraba   pasaba   quería
c) era   tendía   iba   tendía   se unían   veía   empuñaba   sabía   podía

Practice 2

1 éramos   salíamos   estamos   salimos
2 leía   era   leo
3 fumaba   fuma
4 solía   vivía   vive   nos vemos
5 creían   protegía   celebraban   se reúnen

Practice 3

1 c **2** d **3** b **4** j **5** g **6** h **7** e **8** i **9** f **10** a **11** n **12** m **13** o **14** l **15** k

Practice 4

1 una   un   un **2** una **3** un   una **4** una   un **5** una   un **6** un **7** un **8** Una   una

Practice 5

1 la **2** el   la **3** el **4** la **5** El **6** el **7** el **8** la

Practice 6

1 que **2** que **3** lo que **4** lo que **5** lo que **6** que   lo que **7** que **8** lo que
9 Lo que   que **10** que   lo que   lo que   que

Practice 7
1 de 2 de 3 que 4 de 5 de 6 que 7 de 8 de 9 de 10 que
Practice 8
1 sino 2 pero 3 sino 4 sino 5 pero
Practice 9
(1) vuelta **(2)** vergüenza **(3)** igual **(4)** disgusto **(5)** cuenta **(6)** gana **(7)** rabia
(8) bofetada
Progress test 5
1 Cuando era más joven, ella iba/solía ir a la iglesia todos los domingos.
2 En la escuela/el colegio, yo tenía miedo de ciertos profesores.
3 Era/Hacía un día espléndido. El sol brillaba, los pájaros cantaban y me sentía
  verdaderamente/realmente feliz.
4 No me gustan los gatos y detesto (a) los perros.
5 Los profesores no ganan mucho dinero.
6 Los dulces son malos para los dientes.
7 ¿Cuántos idiomas hablas/habla usted?
8 ¿Puedo sacar una foto?
9 No sé qué hacer porque no sé qué/lo que ha pasado.
10 Lo que quiero saber es por qué han hecho eso.
11 Es más difícil de lo que se cree.
12 ¡No es mi hijo, sino mi sobrino!
13 ¡Me da igual!/¡Me da lo mismo!/¡Lo mismo me da!
14 ¿Quieres dar un paseo en coche?
15 ¡Me da asco!

UNIT 6

Practice 1
fue movieron fue se registraron provocaron comenzó pereció vio subió
dio entraron hallaron pereció ocurrió se precipitó fue trasladó falleció
provocó

Practice 2
apareció fue acudieron resultaron se repartió consiguió ejecutaron
instalaron se apoderaron se llevó fueron inspiró popularizó

Practice 3
a) era apostaba podía jugaba murió fue abrió llamó
b) se casó se ponía se untaba fue trataba salía
c) estaba decía podía puso dejó despertó se hallaba exclamó me tragué
era

Practice 4
1 e 2 f 3 a 4 h 5 c 6 g 7 b 8 d

Practice 5
1 no 2 no 3 yes (debe de ser) 4 yes (debes de estar) 5 no 6 yes (debe de
haber) 7 yes (debe de ser) 8 no 9 yes (debe de tener) 10 no

Practice 6

1 cambie 2 no change 3 no change 4 salgas 5 no change 6 compre
7 no change 8 haga 9 escriba 10 ayude 11 llame 12 vengan

Practice 7

1 Oiga Dígame 2 Perdone Baje tome 3 mire Suba siga coja 4 trabaje
trate haga deje Siga vuelva 5 Quédese tome Agite 6 se enfade Salga
Márchese Váyase Cálmese Oiga empuje

Progress test 6

1 Dijo que tenía dolor de cabeza y no se sentía muy bien. 2 Al día siguiente se
levantaron muy temprano. 3 El año pasado fui a España y pasé dos semanas
en Huelva. 4 Estuvimos en España durante cinco meses/Estuvimos cinco
meses en España y luego fuimos a Francia. 5 Explicó que estaba muy cansada
y quería descansar. 6 ¿Cuándo la conociste/conoció usted? ¿Hace dos o tres
años? 7 Salió corriendo de la casa. 8 Al verme, sonrió y me estrechó la mano.
9 Quieren que (yo) empiece mañana. 10 ¿Qué quieren que hagamos?
11 ¡Quiero que (usted) abra la/su maleta! 12 Mírelo, pero no lo toque. 13 Pase.
Siéntese, por favor. 14 Ella debe (de) tener hambre. 15 ¡Empecemos desde el
principio!

UNIT 7

Practice 1

1 Tira Tirad 2 Empieza Empezad 3 Piensa Pensad 4 Corre Corred
5 Vuelve Volved 6 Ten Tened 7 Escribe Escribid 8 Ven Venid

Practice 2

1 Acuéstate 2 Lávate 3 Ponte 4 Quítate 5 Cállate 6 te enfades 7 te vayas
Quédate 8 te burles 9 te muevas 10 te hagas

Practice 3

1 No lo pongas aquí. 2 No lo hagas ahora. 3 No lo comas. 4 No te acerques.
5 No me hables así. 6 No me empujes. 7 No me esperes. 8 No te sientes allí.

Practice 4

deja Pídele observa hazlo dile Toma colócala baraja hazlo divide
coloca extiende examina

Practice 5

Aries: Estarás tomarás sorprenderás renovarás
Tauro: Podrás Empezarás cambiarás Harás liberarás
Virgo: Tendrás saldrás
Libra: conocerás descubrirás
Capricornio: Empezarás te sentirás

Practice 6

1 Si yo lo encuentro, te lo daré. 2 Si ella toma esta medicina, se sentirá mejor.
3 Yo te perdonaré/perdono si me prometes que nunca volverás a hacerlo.
4 Si usted sigue con sus amenazas, llamaré a la policía. 5 Si algún día tengo
suficiente dinero, yo compraré una casita en el campo.

Practice 7

1 Les visitaremos pasado mañana. **2** Lo harán esta tarde. **3** Estoy seguro de que Juan nos ayudará. **4** Tu padre te contará una historia. **5** Han prometido que lo terminarán pronto.

Practice 8

1 reaccionará   se entere **2** aprenderá   vaya **3** mandaré   llegue **4** seguiré   dé
5 seguirá   pueda

Practice 9

1 voy **2** vayas **3** tenga **4** está **5** tenga **6** regrese **7** pueda **8** llega **9** salga
10 tenemos **11** siga **12** hago

Practice 10

1 h (compres) **2** a (salga) **3** g (se queme) **4** i (sea) **5** b (te marches)
6 c (cuides) **7** j (devuelvas) **8** d (se entere) **9** f (lleguen) **10** e (llueva)

Practice 11

1 a/b/d **2** b/c/d **3** b **4** a/d

Practice 12

1 ¿Quién te lo mandó? **2** ¿Me la prestas? **3** ¿Quieres que te lo muestre? **4** Se lo ofrecieron a él. **5** ¡No se los enseñes a ella!

Progress test 7

1 Lo haré más tarde si tengo tiempo. **2** Dice que lo hará cuando tenga tiempo.
3 Si llegamos antes de las ocho, podremos coger el (tren) rápido. **4** Te llamaremos en cuanto/tan pronto como lleguemos. **5** Esperaremos aquí hasta que deje de llover. **6** Voy a darte un mapa para que no te pierdas. **7** Llámala ahora para que sepa que estás bien. **8** No me llames a menos que/a no ser que sea realmente urgente. **9** Siempre que/Con tal que el tren salga a tiempo, estaré/llegaré allí a las ocho. **10** Normalmente/Generalmente salgo muy temprano, antes (de) que se levanten los otros. **11** ¡No toques esa máquina! **12** Se puso rojo cuando ella le dijo que le quería. **13** Se hizo rico y famoso. **14** Se ha vuelto arrogante y vaga/perezosa. **15** Es su libro. ¡Dáselo!

UNIT 8

Practice 1

1 se habían marchado **2** habían robado **3** habían pasado **4** había comido
5 había dormido **6** había viajado **7** había oído **8** habían escondido **9** había gastado **10** había tenido

Practice 2

1 que **2** como **3** que **4** que **5** como **6** que **7** como **8** como **9** como **10** que

Practice 3

1 La Scala es el más famoso teatro de ópera de Italia y uno de los más famosos del mundo. **2** Dijo que era la mejor película que jamás había visto. **3** ¡Hoy es el día más feliz de mi vida! **4** La pitón reticulada es el reptil más largo. Es más larga que seis bicicletas puestas en fila. **5** Hace millones de años, los caballos no eran mayores que los gatos. **6** Las pirañas viven en los ríos de América del Sur y son más peligrosas que los tiburones. **7** El Empire State Building, de Nueva York, es uno de los edificios más altos del mundo. **8** Andorra es uno de los países más pequeños del mundo. **9** El guepardo es el más rápido de los animales que corren. **10** Al oír la noticia, se sintió más feliz que nunca. **11** Cuanto más le doy, más pide. **12** Cuanto más la conozco, (tanto) más la quiero.

Practice 4

1 Ningún **2** ninguna **3** Ninguno **4** ninguna **5** ningún **6** ningún

Practice 5

1 absoluto **2** Ni...ni **3** siquiera **4** nadie **5** tampoco **6** nada **7** ni **8** Nunca más **9** Aún **10** Jamás

Practice 6

1 hervir **2** enfríe **3** le ayude **4** que te diga una cosa **5** que fume **6** que coma carne **7** que hables con él **8** que no viajemos en coche por esa parte del país **9** que estudies otro idioma **10** que busques otro trabajo

Practice 7

1 No digo que tengas que hacerlo. **2** Dudo que (ella) cambie de opinión. **3** No creo que todos los cambios hayan sido positivos. **4** ¡No es cierto/verdad que (ella) te odie! **5** No es cierto/verdad que vayan a despedirte/te vayan a despedir. **6** Quizá/Tal vez estén/están en la cocina. **7** Puede (ser) que se hayan equivocado. **8** Es probable que llueva mañana. **9** Estoy seguro/a de que ella es francesa. **10** No creo que sea española.

Practice 8

1 Mira, hija, más vale que... **2** Será mejor que... **3** correct **4** Es preciso que esto acabe... **5** No es menester que lo hagas... **6** correct **7** correct **8** Me extraña que... **9** Espero que no haya... **10** ¡Que aproveche! (no accent) **11** ...que todo vaya bien. **12** ¡Que lo pases bien!...

Practice 9

1 entienda **2** ...a un abogado que entiende **3** sepa **4** ...a un profesor que sabe **5** sea **6** es **7** tenga **8** sea **9** ...a nadie que pueda **10** ...a nadie que conduzca

Progress test 8

1 Ella dijo que había tenido un accidente. **2** Había llovido durante la noche. **3** No es tan mala como cree todo el mundo. **4** Es tan gordo que apenas puede caminar. **5** No tengo tantos problemas como ella. **6** Mi hermana menor es más grande que mi hermana mayor. **7** ¡Cuanto antes, mejor! **8** Éste debe (de) ser el restaurante más caro de Madrid. **9** No hay mejor restaurante en Madrid. **10** Éste es el peor regalo que jamás he recibido. **11** Ya no es mi amiga y no quiero verla nunca más/ y nunca más quiero verla/ y jamás quiero volver a verla. **12** No me gusta ninguna de estas camisas. **13** No tengo (ni) el tiempo ni el deseo de verle. **14** No le permiten fumar/que fume en casa. **15** Dudo que

vengan/vayan a venir hoy. **16** Quiera(s) o no quiera(s), tendrá(s) que hacerlo.
17 Es/Será mejor que lo hagas ahora./Más vale que lo hagas ahora. **18** Me
alegro de que les guste. **19** Me extraña/sorprende que no hayan llamado.
20 Busco un hotel que no sea demasiado caro.

UNIT 9

Practice 1
1 e **2** y **3** e **4** y **5** e **6** e **7** e **8** y **9** e **10** y

Practice 2
1 ...llamaría a Juan y se lo diría. **2** ...que trataría de llegar antes de las ocho.
3 ...segura de que a Manuel le gustaría el regalo. **4** ...que intentaría hacer todo
lo posible para arreglar la situación. **5** ...dijo que no habría nadie allí. **6** ...dijo
que lo pensaría.

Practice 3
1 e **2** g **3** d **4** f **5** a **6** h **7** i **8** b **9** j **10** c

Practice 4
a) verías; distinguirías; sería; se moviera/moviese; verías; tuvieras/tuvieses;
verías; verías
b) fuera/fuese; tendrían; tuvieran/tuviesen; serían; hubiera/hubiese; habría;
hubiera/hubiese; habría

Practice 5
1 llamara/llamase **2** quiera **3** suprimiera/suprimiese; fuera/fuese **4** beba; sea
5 explique **6** explicara/explicase **7** espere **8** esperara/esperase **9** cambies
10 cambiara/cambiase

Practice 6
1 Por **2** por **3** por **4** por **5** Para   Para **6** Para   Para **7** Por   por **8** por   por
9 por **10** por

Practice 7
1 quien/el que **2** quien/el que **3** quien **4** quienes **5** la que/la cual/quien
6 quien/al que **7** que/la que/la cual **8** la cual **9** las que/las cuales **10** la cual

Practice 8
1 dieciséis **2** veinte   cien **3** veintiún **4** veintiocho **5** treinta y dos   veintidós
6 cuarenta y ocho **7** setenta y cinco **8** ochenta **9** ciento treinta y una
10 doscientas cincuenta **11** quinientas ochenta **12** ochocientas sesenta y cinco
13 cuatro mil **14** mil novecientos ochenta y dos **15** Tercero **16** treinta millones de

Progress test 9
1 Carmen e Isabel son mis mejores amigas. **2** Dijeron que me ayudarían.
3 Deberían/Debieran/Deben disculparse. **4** ¿Por qué me trata(s) como si
fuera/fuese un niño de cinco años? **5** ¡Ojalá (yo) fuera/fuese tan inteligente
como Miguel! **6** ¡Ojalá tuviera/tuviese el dinero para comprar esa/aquella casa!
(or ¡Si tuviera/tuviese el dinero....) **7** Les pedí que lo hicieran/hiciesen lo antes
posible. **8** Si prestaran/prestasen más atención en clase, aprenderían más.

9 Tocaría mejor el piano si practicara/practicase más. **10** Si dejara/dejase de fumar, se sentiría mejor. **11** Me ofrecieron mil pesetas por el cuadro. **12** Y por eso/por ese motivo/por esa razón no quiero verle. **13** La cita es para el dos de junio. **14** Fue Marta quien/la que nos ayudó más. **15** Nació el primero de agosto de mil novecientos setenta y tres.

UNIT 10

Practice 1
1 d 2 c 3 e 4 a 5 b

Practice 2
1 ¿Qué habrías hecho si hubieras estado en la misma situación?
2 Si me hubieran avisado con tiempo, yo hubiera/habría podido hacer algo.
3 Si hubiesen cogido el tren en vez del autobús, no hubieran llegado tarde.
4 Si hubiéramos sabido la verdad, no le habríamos tratado de esa manera.
5 Si hubieses podido vivir…, te hubieras creído que… .

Practice 3
1 tranquilamente 2 alegremente 3 amargamente 4 cortésmente 5 tristemente
6 atentamente 7 profundamente 8 rápidamente 9 calladamente
10 constantemente

Practice 4
1 con calma 2 con paciencia 3 con cuidado 4 con entusiasmo 5 con cariño

Practice 5
1 en 2 con 3 en 4 de 5 con 6 a 7 con 8 a 9 de 10 con

Practice 6
1 claro 2 contentos 3 fuerte 4 mal 5 atento 6 rápido y cómodo

Practice 7
1 x 2 con 3 en 4 de 5 a a 6 a 7 de 8 de 9 de 10 x 11 en 12 en 13 x
14 a 15 a 16 en 17 a 18 en 19 a 20 a

Practice 8
1 …a mi abuela 2 …a mi hermano 3 …a tu madre 4 …a este señor
5 …a la policía 6 …a mi suegra 7 …a todo el mundo 8 …a Juana
9 …a su hermano 10 ¿A quién quieres más, a tu hijo o a tu hija?

Practice 9
1 a Mis Los míos b míos mis c mía mías
2 a tu El tuyo b tus los tuyos c La tuya
3 a Nuestro El nuestro b Nuestra La nuestra

Practice 10
1 el El 2 x 3 El 4 x 5 La 6 Los

Practice 11
1 x 2 x 3 x x 4 El 5 el el 6 el 7 la 8 x 9 el 10 el

Progress test 10

1 Si ella no lo hubiera/hubiese visto con sus propios ojos, no lo hubiera/habría creído. **2** Si hubiera/hubiese conducido con más cuidado, el accidente no hubiera/habría ocurrido. **3** Si hubiéramos/hubiésemos salido cinco minutos más temprano, no hubiéramos/habríamos perdido el tren. **4** Si me lo hubieras/hubieses dicho antes (or Si me hubieras/hubieses avisado antes), hubiera/habría podido hacer algo (or podría haber hecho algo). **5** No deberías/debieras/debes leer a oscuras. **6** Habló/Hablaba en voz baja para no despertar a los otros/a los demás. **7** Jugaban/Estaban jugando tranquilamente en el jardín. **8** A veces se comporta de un modo muy extraño/de una manera muy extraña. **9** Se negaron a darle el dinero a Pedro. **10** Insiste en/Se empeña en hablar con el dueño. **11** Logramos/Conseguimos animarle a venir con nosotros/a acompañarnos. **12** Quedamos en vernos/encontrarnos a las seis. **13** Vi a Teresa ayer. **14** Necesitamos un médico. **15** Voy a Francia el mes que viene porque quiero aprender (el) francés.

Index

Note: (Ex.) = See Extra Reference Section.